**Text and Floral Design:** Jeanne Ha, AIFD CFD Certified Floral Evaluator/Judge

**Editor:** Bruce Wright

**Photographer:** Bianca Madanat

**Design Assistant:** Rosana Cruz

**Graphic Designer:** Kathleen Dillinger

**Publisher:** Travis Rigby



Ft. Lauderdale, florida
wildflower.media

Printed in China

ISBN: 978-1-7355603-4-2

Wildflower.Media

# *Ready, Set, Design!*

YOUR GUIDE TO BECOMING
AN AWARD-WINNING
FLORAL DESIGNER

**JEANNE HA, AIFD CFD**
CERTIFIED FLORAL EVALUATOR/JUDGE

# Contents

# My Floral Design Journey



I did not start my adult years thinking that I wanted to become a florist or professional floral designer. In college, I studied music. As an undergraduate, I majored in voice. In graduate school, I studied musicology. I had planned to go on to get a doctorate in music history.

But around this time, I realized that I couldn't find any meaning in my studies anymore. I longed for work where I could feel that every day, I was doing something tangible that fills a need, something that would make people happy. I wanted to know that I was contributing to my community—even to humanity.

That's when I started working at my aunt and uncle's little neighborhood flower shop. I helped them to set up the new computer system and the new phone system. As I did so, I learned the names of the different kinds of roses and other flowers. Everything was totally new. I loved working with flowers so much! Who wouldn't?

But what enticed me most was when I learned what flowers could do for the customers. I was astounded by how customers reacted upon seeing the floral designs we created, how they would share their personal stories when they ordered flowers, how their faces brightened as they picked up the fresh flowers for their homes. I witnessed the power of flowers firsthand!

As my aunt and uncle had been planning to retire, my husband and I bought the little shop from them in 2004, without knowing quite what we had signed up for. But I found it very interesting, getting to know what people were looking for: design styles, cultural needs, generational preferences.

My little shop, Park Florist, did well, thanks to my aunt's and uncle's support and, at first, my loyal customers' patience. My aunt told me about this very prestigious group of "real" professional floral designers, called the American Institute of Floral Designers (AIFD). Apparently, they were coming to my town with their big annual conference!

This was exciting, and by then I was pretty confident with my design skills, which I had learned from my aunt. I decided to prove myself with this AIFD test thing! My husband always felt sorry that I didn't get to finish my doctoral degree; he was eager to support me in my effort to get AIFD membership. So, I registered to take my test to become an AIFD member in Washington, DC in 2006.

Although I don't have any photos of them, I remember very clearly the table of five designs that I created for my first PFDE (Professional Floral Design Evaluation), including every single stem insertion—I am not kidding! That's how super focused I was when I designed these pieces, I guess. (Actually, I rarely forget my own designs, whether it is a birthday arrangement for a customer or a very important competition piece that won a big prize).

I called my husband that evening as I finished my table. Looking at other candidates' tables, I felt sure that mine was the best! I knew that my customers would be very happy to receive any of my designs: a design for a teenage girl in the hospital, a gallery-opening floral piece, a bridesmaid's

Design for Land Art project,
Southern Chapter of AIFD, 2020

1969

(OPPOSITE PAGE, CLOCKWISE)

Themed design ("the 1960s") for a wholesale competition, awarded the grand prize, 2019

Floral necklace created for an IFDA (Independent Floral Designers Association) presentation, 2020

Design featured in Jeanne's first book, *Asian Allure*, published 2018

bouquet, a casket-top design. They were beautiful, fresh, and full. So, when I received my test result along with the score sheets, I was confused and in denial: in my first trial, I didn't pass the test.

At this point, I had not yet had the real experience of what AIFD is all about. The testing for prospective AIFD members always takes place right *before* AIFD National Symposium. So, it was only after taking the test for the first time, in 2006, that I attended my first AIFD Symposium, in Washington, D.C.

It was a total shock. It was as if a short-order cook at a hotdog stand signed up to attend the most prestigious culinary show and got to watch the top chefs' cooking firsthand. This is an experience that has been commonly shared by AIFD members about their first Symposium. (Remember that this was before the era of social media, when florists didn't get as much opportunity to see what other florists were doing, especially on a large scale, outside of their own area. Nowadays there is also a lot of inspiration available online, if you put your radar out.)

The next three years were my journey to become a "real" professional florist. I went near and far to learn from renowned teachers and mentors, and they opened my eyes to a new world. To return to the cooking analogy, I re-learned everything, from how to peel potatoes to which wine to pair with a certain dish. When I tested again in 2009, in Kansas City, I was extremely nervous and uncertain whether I was good enough to pass. But I did pass, and I was inducted as an AIFD member in Boston in 2010.

I had worked very hard to learn how to meet the standards for passing the PFDE, studying the principles and elements of design and other requirements. But once I passed the test, I was surprised to realize that, rather than feeling constricted by the "rules," my hard-won knowledge and confidence gave me much more creative freedom. I had absorbed the essence of the rules, and no matter what crazy experiment I tried in my design, it always would keep that solid foundation of design principles and aesthetic standards. That's when I started to share my knowledge and experience through many workshops, classes, presentations, and finally through my own school, Washington Flower School, that I founded in 2010 with my dear friend the late David Shover, AIFD, CFD, AAF, PFCI. I've been teaching what I learned and what I know from my retail florist experience to students, including floral design for special events and floral art.

I also love the business part of being a florist (which is a lot different from how many florists feel!). But in this book, I want to focus on design and share the secret of how I have built my repertoire as a professional florist.

In the pathway of professional development, a floral designer has this in common with an opera singer: As a budding soprano, you perfect your technique by studying the roles that are best fitting to your voice. Then, you can expand your repertoire, one role at a time. As a floral designer, you want to gain a solid foundation in basic principles. You also want to develop your own signature style—and the best way to do both of those things is by practicing and refining your own original designs: the designs that you can do best. Then, you are ready to expand your range in any direction, always growing in creative strength.

I hope my story inspires you and helps you to find your own voice as a professional floral designer.

—Jeanne Ha AIFD, CFD

# Who This Book Is For

If you are a floral designer who wants to achieve a higher level of professional skill and professional recognition, this book is for you.

In it, I share a method that I have used myself, and that I have also shared with students at my school. This method can help designers improve their skill and confidence by developing a repertoire of ideas that are original and creative, but also tested and versatile.

Specifically, the method was originally created to help floral designers prepare for the testing process that they will undergo in order to achieve professional certification and accreditation, and also for participation in floral design competitions. Both situations usually involve a "surprise package" as perhaps the most stressful and demanding component.



But the value of the method extends beyond these two challenges (in-person evaluation and floral design competitions). Anybody who has worked in a commercial florist business can agree that in that setting, whether it is a full-service retail flower shop or a studio geared to weddings and events, your daily challenge is actually a kind of surprise package design test.

You might work at an artisan bouquet shop that requires you to create a custom design for each order. Your daily job is then to meet or exceed demands similar to those of a "surprise package" design challenge. Whether you are the person who's ordering fresh flowers and supply materials for your shop, or a designer who needs to work with the materials ordered by someone else, you don't order flowers every time you have a new order or project. You work with what you have in your cooler and on your shelves to meet customers' requests.

Or perhaps you work as a line chef at a very busy high-volume retail shop that handles lots of recipe designs (designed by your senior designer and offered on the website for customers to order). Your job is to copy those recipe designs. Still, you have a challenge as you copy them, as often you have to substitute ingredients. Substitution is not a simple A to B proposition. You need to understand the key points of the recipe design in order to recreate it successfully.

So, everything you do as a professional floral designer amounts to giving the best performance you can, under "surprise package" conditions. That's why practice and study with this book will empower you as a seasoned professional floral designer.

Here is what different kinds of floral design professionals can expect to take away from this book.

**Beginners:** Even though this book is intended mainly for experienced designers preparing to enter a competition or to take the PFDE (Professional Floral Design Evaluation) in order to qualify for professional credentials from AIFD (the American Institute of Floral Designers), it can also give beginners a practical understanding of how professional floral designers plan their designs.

**Teachers:** This book provides a thorough curriculum to prepare students for competition and professional evaluations.

**Experienced designers:** Sharpen your skills and unleash your creativity by reviewing the principles and elements of design and practicing their application, using our proven method.

**Designers preparing for testing or competition:** This book is exactly what you need right now. Your page-by-page journey through the book will give you confidence that you are fully prepared for the task. The organization by category allows you to focus (hardest) on the categories where you think you need the most preparation.

**Evaluators and judges:** This book will provide you with a useful reference regarding what to look for, both in technical terms and in terms of creative flair.

Design for Land Art project, Southern Chapter of AIFD, 2020

Bridal bouquet created for
a contest with the theme,
Hawaiian Tropical Nouveau

CHAPTER 1

# Pathways to Professionalism

In the United States, and in many other countries as well, you can start working as a floral designer and even start your own business without any professional accreditation. Good courses in floral design and business are out there, usually geared to beginners. But in fact, many people embark on a retail floral career without any training whatsoever. They learn as they go.

Over time, however, florists and designers who aspire to a higher level of artistry and success usually recognize the value that lies in seeking professional credentials. It must be said that such credentials are not widely recognized by the general public. Tacking some initials on after your name may not automatically bring you more business. But in the process of earning those initials, you get to see and walk towards new opportunities.

Working toward accreditation elevates you from a line cook to a sous-chef. Once you achieve accreditation, you can set your sights on becoming an executive chef in a five-star restaurant. I am not saying that accreditation by itself gets you all the way toward such a lofty goal. It is only a step along the path. But the skills, knowledge and experience that you acquire through the process will open new doors for you.

A professional florist must be able to create designs that will be pleasing, not only to your own eyes, but also to the eyes of others. Yes, you have a vision of beauty that you seek to realize in your floral compositions. To achieve this, however, your intentions must be clearly communicated. This is what accreditation means: the ability to design for the eyes of others.

Of course, the floral industry's accreditation programs are not only about design. The best ones cover all aspects of the job: terminology, botanical studies, care and handling of fresh materials, practical and technical matters along with aesthetic standards and artistic perspectives. Learning about all of these is what guarantees your growth as a true professional floral designer.

Professional accreditation is a journey—one that continues after you have reached the destination.

## ACCREDITING ORGANIZATIONS

*American Institute of Floral Designers™*

Without a doubt, the American Institute of Floral Designers™ (AIFD®) is the floral industry's leading non-profit organization committed to establishing and maintaining higher standards in professional floral design. With nearly 1,300 members worldwide, AIFD and its members are in the forefront of the industry in presenting educational and design programs.

Accredited membership in AIFD is selective. To be accepted, a candidate must demonstrate advanced professional ability with an intense evaluation program called PFDE® (Professional Floral Designer Evaluation™).

Design featured in Jeanne's first book, *Asian Allure*, published 2018

Each July, successful candidates are inducted into membership during ceremonies at AIFD's acclaimed National Symposium. Considered the most important design event in the floral industry, National Symposium attracts designers, educators and interested individuals from all corners of the world.

You are expected to prove yourself as an exceptional floral designer through the PFDE process. When you think you are ready, the first step is to register yourself as a PFDE candidate on the AIFD website. You will receive a copy of *The AIFD Guide to Floral Design: Terms, Techniques, and Traditions.* This text should be studied to review for Part 1 of the PFDE, the online test.

Registration is open each year from February till mid-April. The on-site design test (Part 2 of the PFDE) is always held in early July, right before AIFD National Symposium.

AIFD also offers another credential, Certified Floral Designer (CFD®). There are three ways to earn this designation, one of which is to participate in the same PFDE as those trying to obtain their AIFD membership. More information about both designations is available on AIFD's website, *www.aifd.org.*

## OTHER CERTIFICATION PROGRAMS

A number of state and regional florist associations sponsor educational programs which, when completed, offer professional credentials. One of the best-known examples is the Professional Certified Florist® (PCF) Program created and managed by the Texas State Florists Association (TSFA).

To earn the PCF designation, applicants must complete each of ten courses, covering business topics as well as design, and pass a written final exam. There is no in-person design evaluation, except as part of the floral-design classes. Rather, completion of the PCF entitles the participant to enroll in TSFA's national certification prep course, with the objective of taking AIFD's PFDE.

Design featured in Jeanne's first book, *Asian Allure*, published 2018

Likewise, the Michigan-based Great Lakes Floral Association (GLFA) sponsors a Certified Florist (CF) program. This program concludes with both a written test and a hands-on design exam, which can be taken online via Zoom.

Other state and regional florist associations also offer certification opportunities. Some are more active than others in maintaining their certification programs, but, in the past, associations with such programs have included Arkansas, Arizona, California, Florida, Georgia, Illinois, Maine, North Carolina, South Dakota, and, on the regional (multistate) level, the Floral Association of the Rockies (covering Colorado and Wyoming) and the Wisconsin and Upper Michigan Florist Association (WUMFA).

Certificate programs in floristry are likewise available from many higher-education and career schools, public and private. While the requirements for obtaining any of these professional credentials may or may not include a "surprise package," design studies are almost always based on the classic principles and elements of design and guided by standards that aspire to those set for AIFD membership.

## FLORAL DESIGN COMPETITIONS

Design competitions and contests take place throughout the year, hosted by industry associations and suppliers including local wholesalers. Designers may progress from competing at the local, state and regional level to national and international competitions, such as the Sylvia Cup, hosted by Professional Floral Communicators - International (PFCI) during the annual convention of the Society of American Florists (SAF), or the FTD World Cup.

By participating in such competitions, you are sure to experience tremendous growth in your knowledge and skills. This is how most of the industry's best-known, high-profile designers were able to step up to the next level of their career.

It may take courage to enter your first competition. But once you get a taste, you will immediately be hungry for more. The process is so much fun. You throw yourself into a situation where you have to create your own, unique floral design, within the given guidelines and limitations, such as theme, choice of vessel, or size. You may be asked to create something sellable or something purely for art's sake. In the most popular and exciting competitions, you go to the competition with only your tool belt, and you are provided with a surprise package of both fresh materials and supplies. The format is basically that of AIFD's PFDE. Within a limited time, you are asked to create several designs by category. The categories will be announced during the initial briefing session. The specifics may vary, but in general they will include a wedding design, flowers to wear, a sympathy tribute, and a designer's choice design. You might have years of experience, but you cannot just walk into the surprise-package situation with a blank mind. This is where the method presented here can work brilliantly!

The immediate goal of this book is to help designers prepare for the surprise package, whether in competition or as part of an in-person evaluation. But, just as competitions and credentials represent a step on the path toward wider goals, in the same way, the method that is explained and explored here can also help working designers meet the "surprise package" challenges that are likely to arise every day in a flower shop or in any kind of floral retail business.

CHAPTER 2

# Sketch & Score

For professional floral designers, as we have seen, learning to perform well in a "surprise package" situation is key to success and advancement. But how do you prepare for a surprise?

Actually, many things about the typical surprise package are predictable. These can be prepared for and, most important, practiced in advance. Whether in a floral design competition, in a hands on evaluation, or in daily florist practice, certain basic types of design are required again and again. The surprise component is all about the materials that you will have at hand, along with, perhaps, finer points of expression dictated by the particular person or occasion for whom, hypothetically, you are creating a design.

The way to improve your readiness, then, is:

**Learn to think schematically**, so that your design is patterned on a template, one that you can fill in with whatever materials are available.

**Learn how to be flexible and adaptable**, tweaking your template to both the materials and the overall mood or style you want to achieve.

**Learn to evaluate, and constantly re-evaluate**, both your template and your finished designs, using commonly accepted standards that can help you achieve objectivity. A score sheet based on the principles and elements of design can encourage you to consider all of the different parameters that work together in a truly successful floral design.

By following the method introduced here, you can achieve all of these goals and grow confident in your ability to meet any floral design challenge that may present itself. First, you study and create a variety of design templates to fit different needs and occasions. Having mastered this foundational repertoire, you can then advance to the highest levels of creativity.

## HOW THE METHOD WORKS

The concept is simple:

**Begin with a sketch.** It doesn't matter if you don't think you are good at sketching. That's a skill that will improve as you practice. But the goal here is not to make a beautiful sketch, but rather, to create a template, an outline, that shows the "bones" of your design.

You may fill in details indicating the actual flowers you plan to use for the initial design. But what's important about the sketch is that you let it be guided by the principles and elements of design. How are you planning to establish the focal area? What are the main lines in the design? Does it achieve both physical and visual balance? Are all the elements of the design appropriate in scale? For example, is your bouquet scaled to the size of the container, and vice versa?

While a sketch is two-dimensional and probably limited to black and white, at this stage you also want to be thinking about depth, color, and texture.

**Use a scoring sheet** to evaluate your sketch and make any revisions necessary. (More about scoring and scoring sheets in the next chapter.)

**Create a design** based on the revised sketch, and again, evaluate using a scoring sheet. Now you have an opportunity to add mechanics to the criteria you score.

**Finally, create more designs** (at least one or two) based on the same template, but using completely different materials. And of course, re-evaluate the completed designs. You don't need to make a new sketch. In real life, you wouldn't have the opportunity to do so.

You may well end up with a different color scheme and stylistic effect. The underlying structure may require some adaptation for the sake of balance and scale. But that's the point: you are learning to be responsive to your floral materials, while using them in a way that serves a larger vision for your design, its shape, proportion, visual balance and flow.

## HOW TO USE THIS BOOK

In this book, you see template sketches. You should make your own sketches, for the sake of practice, but it's fine if they are basically copies of these. There's nothing wrong with copying; in fact, this is a proven method for learning. Bach learned the techniques of musical composition by copying his predecessors' music; that's also how he taught his sons and students.

Design created for presentation at Portland, Oregon's Lan Su Chinese Garden, 2018

First copy, then create original sketches and designs. Stick to basic structures, however, and always design your templates with substitutable materials in mind.

Don't time yourself at this stage. Your goal is that eventually you will be able to produce creative, competitive, professional-quality designs in a time-limited situation. But for now, just focus on getting high scores with your sketches and designs.

It is essential that you apply the method to every design format presented here, using your own hands, rather than just flipping through the book and saying, "Oh, I know how to do that." Begin by copying. Then, as you gain in practice and grow in confidence, you can modify the designs and add your own ideas as well.

CHAPTER 3

# All About Scoring



Feeling nervous about scoring? It goes without saying that the scores you give your own designs may not be the same as a professional evaluator's. Indeed, there is always a subjective element to scoring, and professional evaluators also differ in their scores.

Especially at the beginning, you may wish to ask a more experienced designer, or a qualified professional evaluator, if you happen to know one that you can call on, for an independent score. In a flower shop, employees could also be encouraged to score each other's daily work from time to time, as a fun and instructional group activity.

In the long run, however, it's important to practice scoring your work on your own. As you continue with it, you will gain in perception and proficiency.

The key to successful self-evaluation is to understand that each and every design that you create for a test or competition will be judged using the same design criteria, based on the principles and elements of design, with the same importance given to each. Judges are not allowed to evaluate the overall design generally. Nor can the score for one design criterion affect the others.

For example, a judge may give a design 3 out of 5 for focal emphasis, because he or she perceives that the focal area in the composition is not as strong as it could be. The judge may also give the same design a score of 5 out of 5 for line movement. What she cannot do is to allow one score to influence another. The final score is calculated by adding all the others together.

With each design, then, you need to show your full creativity and strength in all criteria. If your wedding bouquet earns very strong marks for color, harmony, depth, mechanics, and focal emphasis, but no points at all for line, you will not be in a good competitive position with this design.

We all know that in some design categories, it is harder than in others to achieve strong line, or focal, or depth, etc. But that is something you can prepare for in advance. Every designer has a hard time achieving depth in a corsage. Therefore, if you have practiced that particular challenge ahead of time, your corsage design will stand out to the evaluators' eyes. Everyone has trouble creating line in a hand-tied bridal bouquet. But, if you have a sketch in mind that solves that problem, you have a leg up on your competition.

## PRINCIPLES AND ELEMENTS

Most of the criteria that are used in judging and evaluating are based on the principles and elements of design. Therefore, a basic understanding of these principles and elements is essential to the scoring process.

Very briefly, the principles are the aesthetic guidelines that should govern the organization of a design, such as balance, contrast and rhythm. The elements are the aspects of a design that can be directly observed, such as line, color, and texture.

This book is not meant to be an in-depth guide to the principles and elements. There are many books and online resources that can serve this purpose—among them, *The AIFD Guide to Floral Design: Terms, Techniques, and Traditions,* available for purchase on the AIFD website. To understand how the principles and elements are used in judging, I also strongly recommend the book, *A Fresh Look at Judging Floral Design* by Hitomi Gilliam AIFD and Kathy Whalen AIFD.

However, I will share the following questions you can ask yourself in scoring your own designs, geared to the criteria that are typically used in judging.

First, in relation to the principles of design:

**Proportion and Scale:**
Is the overall size of your design, both height and width, pleasingly proportioned to the container?

Is the length of your lines in scale for the overall size of your composition?

Is the proportion of different colors pleasing and well balanced?

Are blooms of different sizes used in pleasing proportions (versus using blooms that are all, or almost all, of the same size)?

**Balance:**
Is your design physically and visually balanced?

For your long lines, large-headed flowers, and dark-colored flowers, did you create any counterbalance?

**Dominance and focal area:**
Dominance is the design principle that encompasses emphasis, including the focal area, and accent. Most important in scoring is to look at the focal area.

Is the focal area established strongly?

What technique or techniques did you use to bring attention to your focal area? If you created your focal area with grouping of roses in a color that contrasts with the flowers or foliage around it, then that's a good focal area, but not yet established with a creative flair. Options for drawing attention to the focal area could be, sheltering the area with leaves elevated on their stems or with umbrellas woven out of grass, or terracing the focal area materials to create layers.

Is your focal point accented by contrasting or transitional accompanying materials?

Is there any other area in the design that makes it unclear which is the primary focal area? Don't create any possible ambiguity with a competing, secondary focal area, however tempted you may be by your beautiful material. Other than the materials in your focal area, everything else in the design needs to point to and accentuate it.

**Rhythm and depth:**
Rhythm is the principle that includes repetition, transition, and depth. For now, let's talk about depth, and begin with your focal area:

Does your focal area "indent"? You want your focal area flowers to come out further than other flowers.

Did you also create depth in the placement of your basing materials, with different levels of height? Terracing and shadowing are useful techniques here.

How have you placed your tallest materials? Even in a one-sided design, avoid putting them all in the very back, so that they create a flat wall. This might cause everything else in front of the wall also to look quite flat.

Did you create any negative space (empty space that is nonetheless perceived as part of the design)?

**Unity:**
Does any element of your design seem not to belong, not to go with the rest? Do the flowers comport well with the container? Does everything add up, so that the whole is greater than the individual parts?

Next, the elements of design. If anything, these are even more important in judging, because they are somewhat less subjective, more tangible and obvious for the judges to see. Tackle these to get a high score that no one can argue with:

**Line:**
Do the line or lines you have created have a strong, visible presence?

What materials and techniques have you used to create line movement in the design? If you created your strong primary line and secondary line with line flowers exclusively, that will look good, but it may not get you the perfect score you want. Consider other materials and techniques for creating line movement in your design. Enhancement with wire, or tailoring, binding, and manipulation of foliage will show more skill and creativity than simply using line flowers. Step forward to your perfect score!

If you have static lines, did you enhance them to create some rhythm? If you create a strong static line with your flowers and then establish a dynamic line as a contrast to that, it will lend more artistic flair to your composition and earn you more points.

Is there anything else that competes with your main lines?

Do your lines lead the eye to your focal area? If you did everything to create beautiful lines, but they point somewhere other than to your focal area, it will take points from your line score.

**Color:**
What kind of color harmony did you use? Be aware of your color strategy and use it consistently.

Did you repeat your colors with different materials? If you used different colors, did you also use any materials in transitional colors to connect them? There is a lot more you can learn about principles (primary and secondary) and elements of design. Color alone is a fascinating study that can energize your perception and skill. But remember, the real value of these terms and concepts comes as you learn to apply them in your creative work. That you can only accomplish by doing.

## MECHANICS

In addition to the principles and elements, mechanics is almost always among the criteria that appear on the judges' scoring sheet. Here what's important is to avoid mistakes that could lose points.

Is any floral foam visible? This is the first thing some judges and evaluators (including myself!) will check, because it's very easy to observe and a very obvious reason for deducting points. The best method to make sure all your foam is hidden—and I mean all—is to hide it before you begin any other insertions. Afterthoughts tend to show.

Is any plastic visible? This means plastic utility containers, bouquet holders, foam cages, casket saddle bases, etc.

Is any non-decorative wire visible? Green floral wire, or any wire that does not have a decorative purpose like aluminum or paper-wrapped binding wire, should be hidden.

Is any glue visible? When you first apply cold glue, it's hard to tell what will show up later; it leaves a yellow stain only after it dries. Make sure you have applied glue only to surfaces that won't show.

Is your binding and wire work clean and meticulous? It should look as if machine-made. Check for sloppy details, such as leaving a banded wire end not cleanly cut. Are your bindings finished cleanly and the same throughout the composition?

Last but not least, are all of your flowers well hydrated and able to drink from a water source? In some cases, an evaluation of your work may not take place until the following day. Pay particular attention to any fragile, wilt-sensitive flowers.

# A SAMPLE SCORING SHEET

A downloadable sample scoring sheet, of the kind used by evaluators in AIFD's Professional Floral Design Evaluation, is available on the AIFD website, *www.aifd.org*. This sample allows for scoring five design categories on one sheet (sympathy, wedding, arrangement, designer's choice, and flowers to wear).

| | WEDDING DESIGN | SYMPATHY DESIGN | FLOWERS TO WEAR | DESIGNER'S CHOICE | ARRANGEMENT |
|---|---|---|---|---|---|
| Category Interpretation or Creativity | 1-2-3-4-5 | 1-2-3-4-5 | 1-2-3-4-5 | 1-2-3-4-5 | 1-2-3-4-5 |
| Color (Harmony, Balance) | 1-2-3-4-5 | 1-2-3-4-5 | 1-2-3-4-5 | 1-2-3-4-5 | 1-2-3-4-5 |
| Line (Movement, Rhythm) | 1-2-3-4-5 | 1-2-3-4-5 | 1-2-3-4-5 | 1-2-3-4-5 | 1-2-3-4-5 |
| Scale and Proportion | 1-2-3-4-5 | 1-2-3-4-5 | 1-2-3-4-5 | 1-2-3-4-5 | 1-2-3-4-5 |
| Focal Emphasis or Dominance | 1-2-3-4-5 | 1-2-3-4-5 | 1-2-3-4-5 | 1-2-3-4-5 | 1-2-3-4-5 |
| Balance (Physical and Visual) | 1-2-3-4-5 | 1-2-3-4-5 | 1-2-3-4-5 | 1-2-3-4-5 | 1-2-3-4-5 |
| Depth | 1-2-3-4-5 | 1-2-3-4-5 | 1-2-3-4-5 | 1-2-3-4-5 | 1-2-3-4-5 |
| Texture | 1-2-3-4-5 | 1-2-3-4-5 | 1-2-3-4-5 | 1-2-3-4-5 | 1-2-3-4-5 |
| Mechanics | 1-2-3-4-5 | 1-2-3-4-5 | 1-2-3-4-5 | 1-2-3-4-5 | 1-2-3-4-5 |
| Unity or Harmony | 1-2-3-4-5 | 1-2-3-4-5 | 1-2-3-4-5 | 1-2-3-4-5 | 1-2-3-4-5 |
| Category Total | __/50 | __/50 | __/50 | __/50 | __/50 |



The AIFD website also gives the following explanation of how to determine the number of points that should be assigned to a given design along any of the individual Design Evaluation criteria:

| 5 Excellent | 4 Above Average | 3 Average | 2 Below Average | 1 Not Acceptable |
|---|---|---|---|---|
| Exceptional use of design principles and elements with strong creative emphasis | Good consistent application of design principles and elements with a creative flair | Good design work, applying use of the principles and elements of design, but not demonstrating any special flair or creative emphasis | Weak in the application of design principles and elements and creativity, would not qualify as a good basic design | Design work lacking the application of the principles and elements of design and shows no creativity |

22

CHAPTER 4

# Formal Linear Design

What is formal linear design? It's not likely to show up as a category on its own in the "surprise package" portion of a competition or evaluation session. Nor is it a term that customers usually use in making requests!

Nonetheless, formal linear design is the default design style you should know and understand well in order to achieve high scores, both with judges and with customers. It applies to all categories of design.

In competition and testing, assigned categories may be more broadly or more specifically defined. You could be asked to create a centerpiece, a hospital design, a party design, a presentation design. The occasion, recipient, or style could also be further specified, for example: "asymmetrical triangle arrangement for a sympathy gift for the home," "hospital arrangement for a teenage girl," "arrangement for a business opening with parallel stem placements," "arrangement for an art gallery."

You may also be given more freedom with a category called "designer's choice." Whatever the assignment, you need to pay attention to its specific terminology and requirements. But once you have done that, in nearly every case, your best bet is to create a formal linear design.

Formal linear design is a highly versatile design style. Even more important, formal linear design allows you to truly showcase, in one design, every single one of the principles and elements of design. In other styles, perhaps you can feature fabulous line, but it's harder to create a strong focal area. Or perhaps you can achieve perfect form, but line value is lacking. In formal linear design, the elements and principles complement rather than compete with each other.

Formal linear design style can be applied to everyday floral gift occasions such as birthday, anniversary, or get well; to sympathy tributes; even to wedding work, such as altar decorations or wedding bouquets.

Within this design style, you have various options at your disposal. You can choose to create a simple vertical design, a horizontal design, an L-shaped design, or another variation on the style. Depending on what materials you have at hand and any other requirements, you can choose the best type of formal linear design to work with.

# ASYMMETRICAL
# FORMAL LINEAR DESIGN

In this book, we will avoid all symmetrical shapes, because they aren't the best forms to earn points in competition or testing when you are looking for adding "creative flair." Instead, our focus will be on asymmetrical formal linear design.

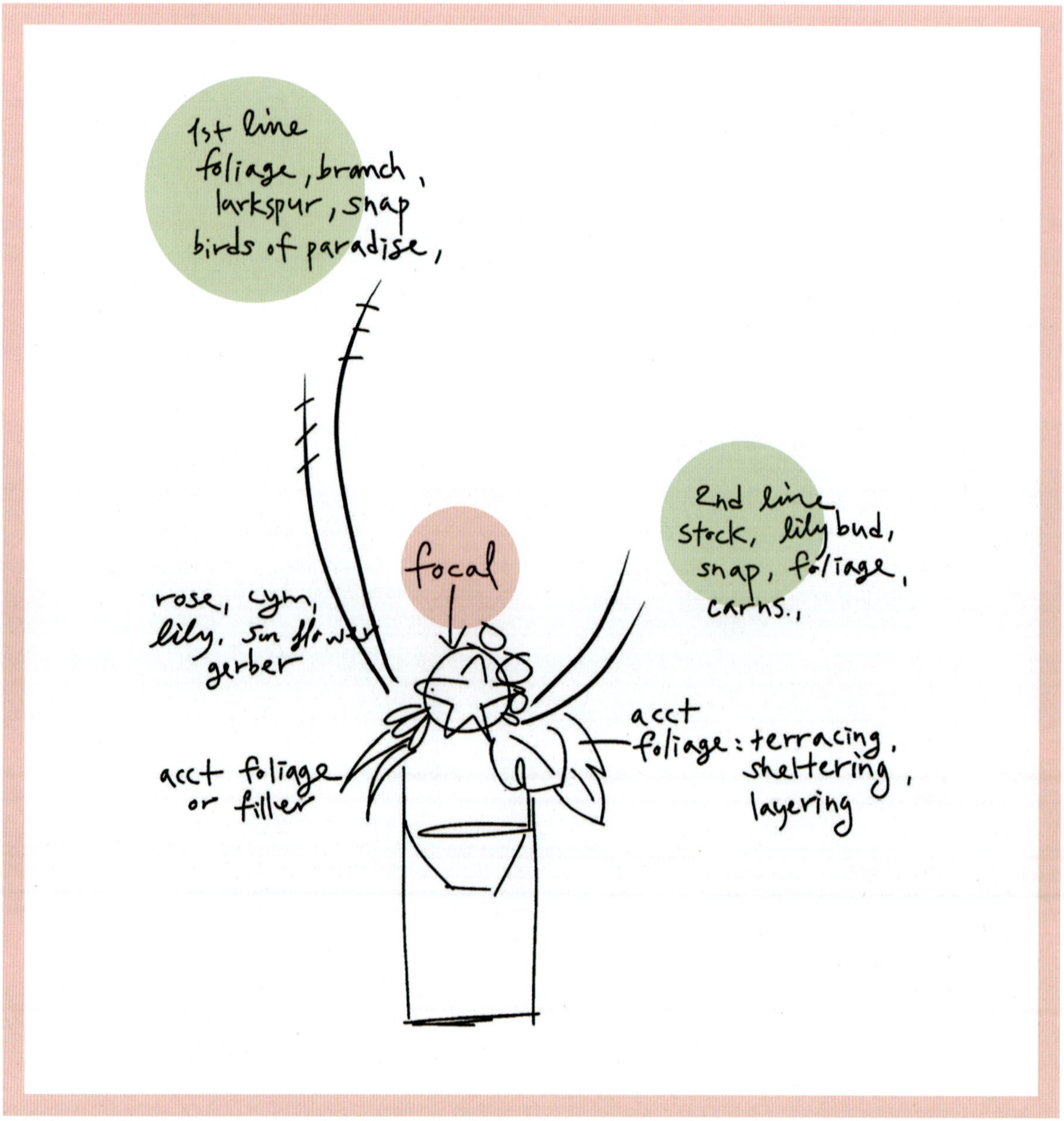




The first step is to create a sketch. It doesn't matter if you think you are good at sketching or not! The idea is to create a template for your design idea that covers the basics: line, focal, visual balance, scale and proportion. First, score the sketch, as best you can without seeing the completed design. Then, create a design based on your sketch and score it as a judge would in a floral design competition. Go back to your sketch and correct anything that brought your score down. Then make another design and score it. Continue with the process until you have a template that can yield a perfect score.

Now that we have a template for an asymmetrical, formal linear design, let's try realizing it three different ways, using different materials. In this first version, the longer, primary line is established with a grouping of pink snapdragons. A second line is created with fuchsia stocks. Within these two main lines, open negative space invites the eye to settle on the focal area—here composed of three terraced, pink gerbera daisies and embellished with loops of variegated lily grass and accents of flat cane. Foliage of various kinds adds depth and balance to the design, while lily buds, hypericum and mini green hydrangea add texture.

## DESIGN TIP

Use the natural curve in Flat Cane to create rounded accents that shelter and float.

A second version of the same design template uses birds of paradise and delphinium for the two main lines. The focal area is done with yellow roses, plus—to pick up the color from the birds of paradise—orange lilies. Croton with its variegated orange and yellow veins is chosen to carry the same color scheme. The design is finished off with eryngium, yarrow, and swirling accents made with Mega Wire.

## DESIGN TIP

Make even curls in decorative wire by wrapping it around a water tube.

The choice of materials gives this third design a very different look, but it is clearly based on the same template. The primary line is created with aspidistra foliage, wired to hold it upright and give it a pleasing curve; the second line with a combination of yarrow and Pear Leaf Natural Wrap, mounted on picks. The focal area showcases plucked sunflowers and green cymbidium orchids, accented with craspedia, croton leaves, white and yellow mums, orange spray roses, and circular medallions made with coiled aluminum wire. Small monstera leaves balance and complete the design, extending the primary line on the other side of the focal area.

## DESIGN TIP

To coil decorative wire, hold it flat between two fingers while you rotate the center with needle-nose pliers.

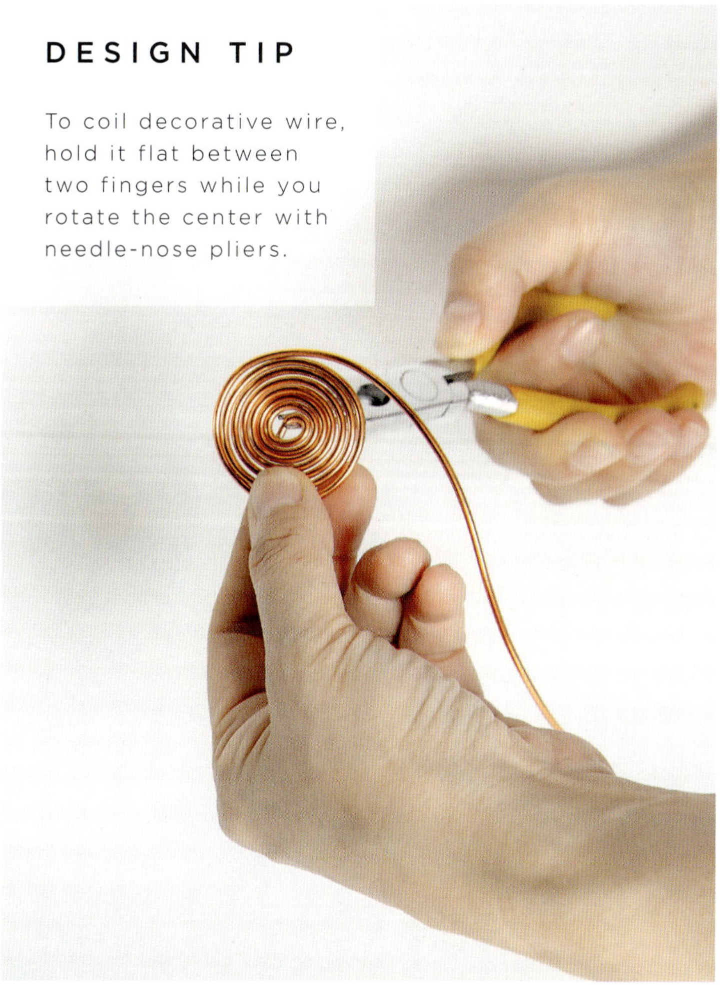

## DESIGN TIP

Rectangular sections of Natural Wrap make beautifully textured accents.

Let's look in greater depth at how you might score another asymmetrical formal linear design. As with those preceding, this design shows why the asymmetrical formal linear style offers a good strategy for scoring high points in all the judging criteria. With a primary and a secondary line, created using different materials and on different levels, the eye naturally is drawn to the focal area that falls in the negative space between them.

Tropical materials in bold colors give this design a strong impact. The primary line on the left is created with birds of paradise foliage, the secondary line on the right with red ginger stems. In the negative space between these lines, the focal area is anchored with groupings of red gerbera daisies, yellow cymbidium orchids, red 'Freedom' roses and red 'Mikado' spray roses.

Both the primary and the secondary lines intersect the focal area and continue with different materials on the other side: the line of the red ginger continues on the other side of the focal area with red anthuriums, while the line of the birds of paradise foliage is extended with trails of Italian ruscus on the right. This X formation provides a solid visual balance to the design.

The bold color harmony of red and yellow makes a very strong statement. It is reinforced by gluing yellow button mums to the centers of the red gerbera daisies—a technique that also adds design interest to the focal area. The gerberas are terraced by inserting them at different heights. The yellow and red combination is repeated in the yellow cymbidium orchid blooms, with their red throats. Red appears also in the variegated anthurium leaves, tucked underneath the roses. Thoughtful and delicate details, like the variegated leaves and the accents with knotted variegated lily grass, offer contrast with the bold style of the design overall.

## DESIGN TIP

The color scheme pops when yellow button mums are glued into red gerberas with floral adhesive.

This design uses the same line structure as the previous design, but it employs different materials: the primary line is again created with bird-of-paradise foliage, while colorful bird-of-paradise blooms form the secondary line. Being spare and simple, the birds of paradise leaves make a strong statement—one that would nonetheless be boring on its own. They are playfully reinforced with craspedia stems and embellished with dynamic, curvy lines created with copper flat wire, which is further decorated with glued-on hypericum berries. The copper wire adds depth as well as line value.

At the center of these lines, 'Free Spirit' orange roses create the focal point. The foliage line is balanced on the other side with 'Xanadu' philodendron foliage, while croton leaves are juxtaposed to the birds of paradise. The beautifully veined croton leaves work as a transitional material that blends and unifies the color scheme of yellow, orange and green. This color harmony is further underlined by the copper wire and the copper accent on the container.

Like others we have featured so far, this design is based on two asymmetrical lines. The solid wide leaf of ginger on the left creates a strong primary line, while the blue delphinium grouping on the right forms a secondary line. These two lines draw the eye down to the focal point where they meet in a cluster of white roses.

What makes this design different is the way the negative space between the two lines is framed with equisetum bridges, which also connects the two lines at the top. Stems of equisetum are folded so that the tips overlap in the middle, where they are bound together with silver flat aluminum wire. The frame, made with materials that bring a different texture, gives extra interest and strong impact to this design.

The color scheme here combines royal blue, purple, and white, with various shades of green, accented with yellow. The line of blue delphinium is complemented on the opposite side with thistle, while the variegated ginger foliage is balanced with green cymbidium blooms and with terraced, dark and shiny aralia leaves.



Various textured materials, including 'Green Trick' dianthus and *Pittosporum tenuifolium*, add interest to the basing. A silver wire orb echoes the silver tone of the banding, enhancing the feeling of unity in the design.

# **VERTICAL** FORMAL LINEAR DESIGN

Formal linear design is a broad and versatile style, within which we can find subcategories such as vertical formal linear design, horizontal design, parallel design, and designs based on triangles or curvy lines. It's helpful to be aware of these strategies and to practice each of them. It's also fun!

The simplest and the most straightforward kind of formal linear design is a vertical design style that emphasizes a single south-north line in the composition. You can create a very strong statement with the main line leading to your focal area.

With that strong single line and focal point, you can also use many design techniques to highlight them with creative flair. Among the possible variations are a) reinforcements to the vertical line, b) foliage that fans out to one side, and c) quickly crafted accents that mediate between the focal and the vertical, connecting them and filling the space in between. As you add to and adapt the basic structure, always check your additions for overall balance, proportion, and unity in the design.

Here we introduce a single template sketch with four fully realized design variations using different materials.

In the first design, the vertical line is created with insertions of river cane, all of the same length. Slightly fanned so that they come together at the focal area, the four stems of river cane together serve as one main vertical line. Burgundy snapdragons lend strength and impact to the line. To add creative flair, the river cane is banded at random points with aluminum wire in a fuchsia color, which is repeated elsewhere in the composition. It reinforces the monochromatic (or closely analogous) color scheme of bluish reds, while adding a different texture.

A single, wide-open 'Starfighter' lily establishes the focal point. The 'Starfighter' is an excellent choice. You don't want to distract from its impact by overembellishing it. And yet—in the context of a competition or professional design evaluation—you would want to go a little beyond the easy and expected.

**DESIGN TIP**

Needle-nose pliers are essential for creating precise shapes with decorative wire.

To score that extra point that you will need to get your design upgraded from average to excellent, you may want to add rather subtle accents, like the wire decorations seen here—petal shapes, added to the back of the lily as though it were a double. Coins made of swirled wire are added to the bloom itself and repeated on the monstera leaves at the side.

When you work with decorative aluminum wire, make sure you hold your needle-nose pliers tightly where you are making angles—in this case, the tip of the petal shape—and bend it tightly so that you have a sharp pointy shape.

The tall vertical lines are anchored, not just with the lily bloom, but also with the two monstera leaves supporting the focal area. They create a bold and simple accent to the design. The two leaves are separated by grouping of fuchsia carnations, so that one appears as a shadow of the other.

Above the lily, crossing over and softening the strong vertical line of the river cane and snapdragon stems, loops of lily grass weave through each other and around the snap-dragons. Without them, the composition might look quite flat.

Here, the natural curve of the yellow snapdragons inspired the placement of some of them slightly off to one side, in a closely fanned formation—but with their tips pointing inward toward the axis. The line of the snapdragon stems, now slightly diagonal, leads the eye down to the grouping of white 'Eskimo' roses that dominates the focal area. This primary line is reinforced with the backing of a single monstera leaf. It flows through the focal area and out at the opposite side below it, where it continues with loops of gold etched wire, backed by calathea leaves.

Sheltering the focal area and softening the transition between it and the descending central line, knotted loops of variegated lily grass take the arched form of cathedral windows. The focal area is further complemented with yarrow and button mums in different shades of yellow, plus hypericum, mini green hydrangea, and pittosporum, completing an analogous color harmony. This is a very clean and simple design statement, featuring a well-balanced, asymmetrical line.

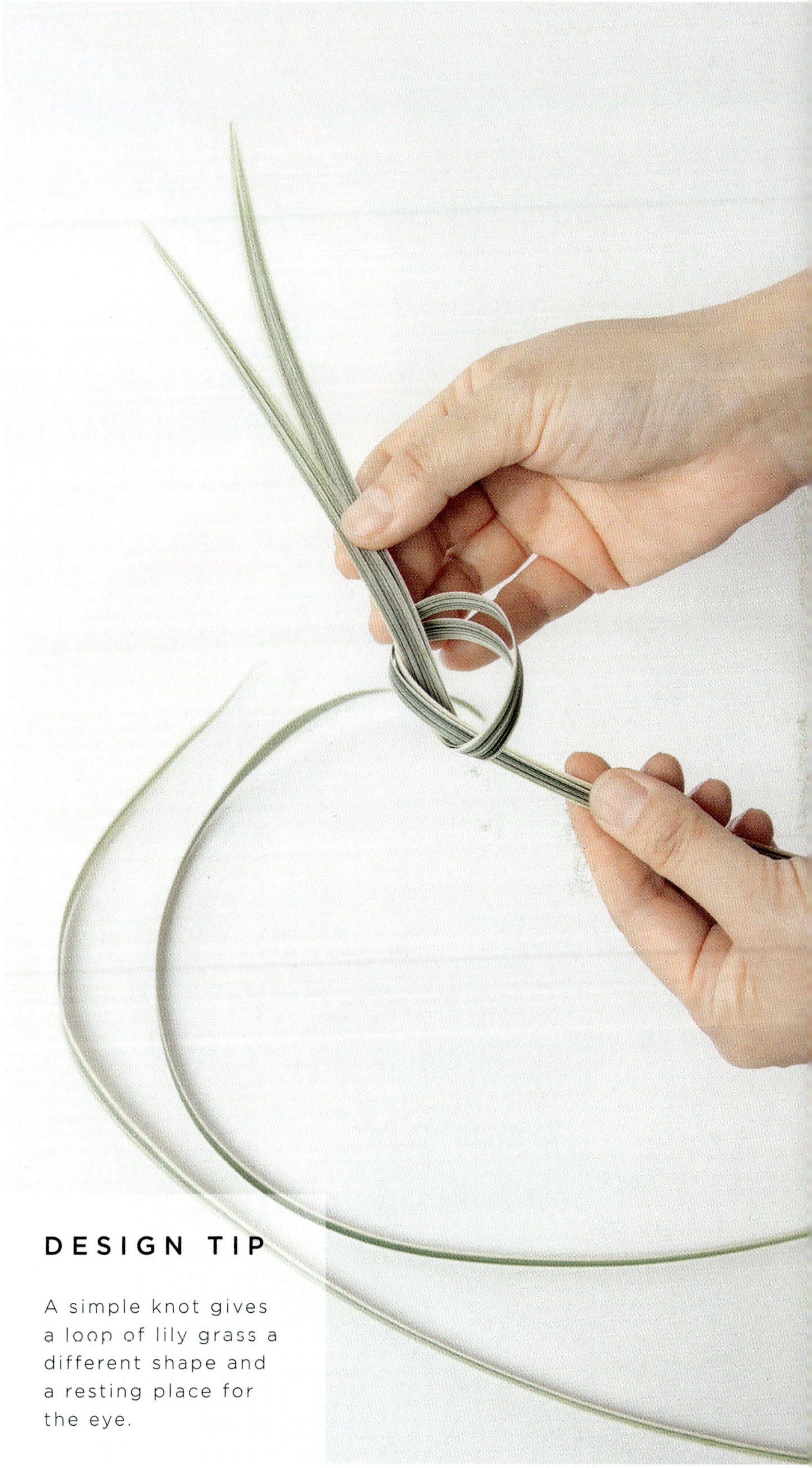

## DESIGN TIP

A simple knot gives a loop of lily grass a different shape and a resting place for the eye.

Once again, a single, wide-open 'Starfighter' lily establishes a very strong focal area, nestled on a cushion of white carnations and flanked with aralia leaves on one side, red anthuriums on the other. 'Freedom' roses define the vertical line, not only with their stems, but also with the implied line that the eye draws from one red rose head to the next. White snapdragons and lily buds back up the roses, adding volume and texture to the design, but their pale hues cannot compete with the vibrant, advancing color, red, and they remain appropriately in the background.

The excitement is punched up with red aluminum wire, fashioned into rectangles that bring the angles of the cube container up among the flowers: a creative touch that adds points for harmony and unity in the design!

## DESIGN TIP

Floral tape secures this wire accent to a wood pick for stable insertion into foam.

Simplicity and sophistication meet in this design: green grasses define a spare vertical line complemented with midollino and equisetum fashioned into sharp, modern angles. The insertion points for the slender grasses form a circle, which lends depth to the design, dimension and transparency to the main vertical line. The repetition of angles, also evident in the square, shallow orange dish that holds the design, brings harmony and unity to the composition.

The color scheme likewise helps to unify the design. Orange (seen in the spray roses and variegated croton leaves) is paired with its complementary color, chartreuse green (anthuriums, cymbidium orchids, the green grass, and the midollino). In the focal area, shadowing of the small monstera leaves and green anthuriums adds depth and weight, anchoring and balancing the design.

# **PARALLEL** DESIGN

In the parallel design style, all materials are inserted upright, at 90 degrees to the container. The style works best with long and narrow containers. It offers an easy way to showcase the taller plant materials—plus, it gives you the opportunity to play with interesting techniques in the basing of the design.

As all the stems need to be inserted parallel to each other, the common mistake we see in this type of design is that your composition may lack a clearly defined focal area. Avoid creating confusion with dual, competing focal areas. You need to establish a strong focal area along with strong lines.

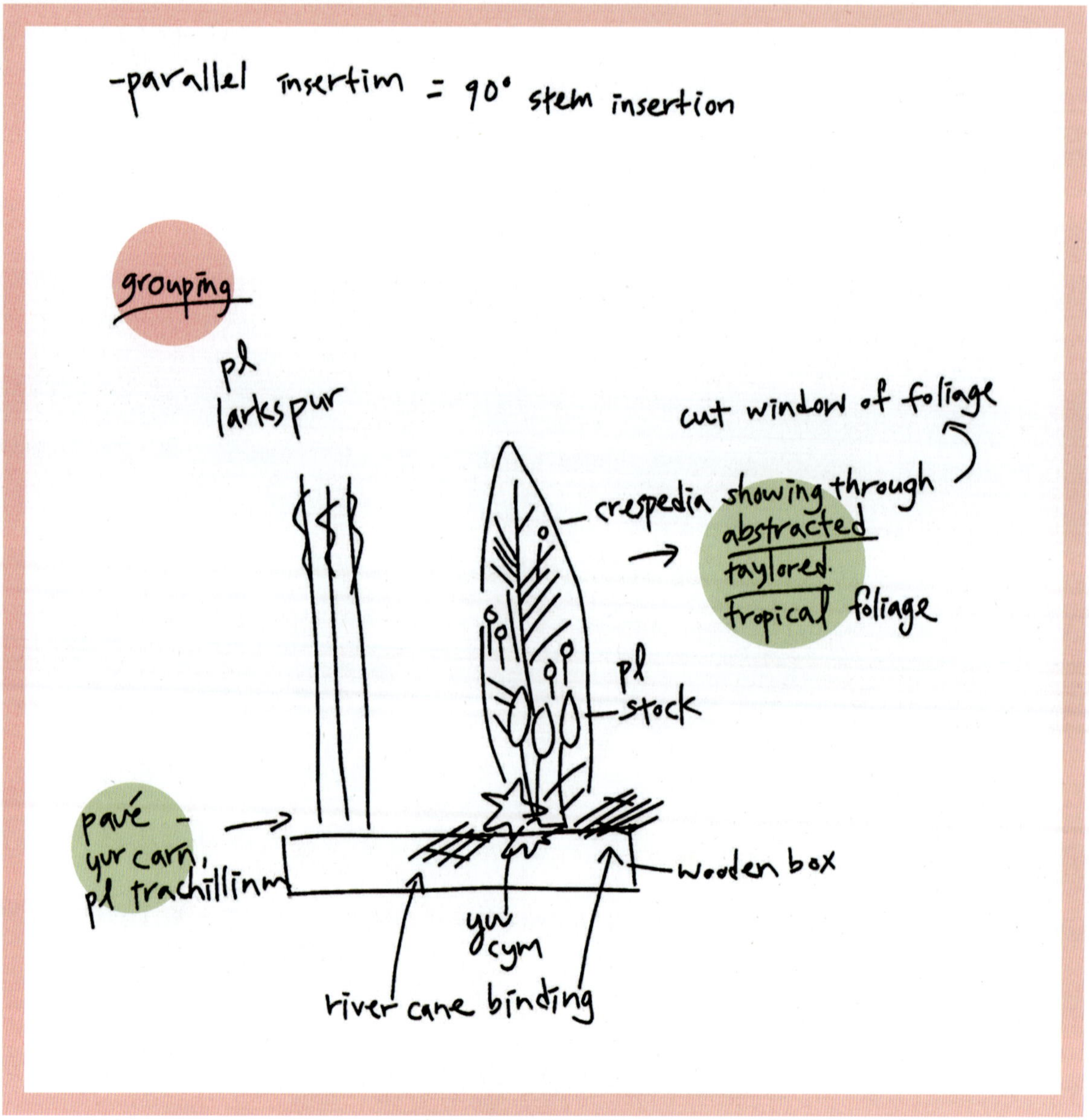


A good sketch template for a parallel design should clearly suggest a primary line and a secondary line. Plan to take advantage of the strengths in this design style to use creative techniques, both in the basing and with your upright stems.

Gladiolus stems work beautifully as primary line in a parallel design, since you have no problem showing all the florets, including wide-open ones at the base of the stem. In the first of our two parallel designs, the primary and secondary lines are clearly differentiated by height and by width. The primary line is more strongly reinforced, with ginger leaves as a backdrop to the gladiolus and a bird-of-paradise bloom added to one side.

## DESIGN TIP

Windows cut in a variegated ginger leaf emphasize its natural veining.



The ginger leaves have been tailored with windows cut from the leaves along the natural veining. These mimic the variegated pattern of the leaves and also lighten their visual weight.

The second line is done with pencil heliconia and purple stock. The two lines are separated by negative space, but they are also connected by the focal point, clearly established with an open Asiatic lily, accented with orange spray roses and green cymbidiums. Other details that enrich the design are the beautifully patterned croton leaves and the layered mini anthurium leaves.

The dominant colors here—orange, purple, and chartreuse green—combine in a color harmony that could be considered as triadic or split complementary. At the base, the orange flowers stand out clearly against a background done almost entirely in chartreuse.

In a second example of parallel design, the main line is announced with green gladiolus, again backed with tailored ginger leaves. The secondary line is done with white snapdragons and yellow craspedia. The focal area is established with a grouping of white lilies, accented with green cymbidiums. A few blue delphiniums have been added, not as line flowers, but simply mixed in for color contrast; they punch up the main color harmony, dominated by yellow, green, and white.

# **HORIZONTAL** DESIGN

Horizontal design might seem like a relatively obscure style, but there are good reasons for practicing your skills and strategy in this type of design. As a professional floral designer, you might well be called upon to create a low-lying design with a strong horizontal line for a specific need—for example, as a centerpiece on a long table at a wedding feast, or for a spot in a client's home on a sideboard, underneath a painting that the client doesn't want obscured.

But this type of design can be appealing for less practical reasons as well. Horizontal lines have a soothing, restful quality. Then again, horizontal designs stand out with creative flair, simply because they are not the norm. In the natural world, flower stems mostly grow straight up—which is why verticals dominate most flower arrangements.

Working with the horizontal design style poses specific creative and technical challenges. And that's a good reason why practicing with this style can help you shine in design competitions or professional evaluations, as well as with your customers.

A horizontal design generally begins with a long, low container—but what if you don't have such a container on hand? This template sketch relies instead on something almost every flower shop keeps in stock: three glass cube containers placed in a row. The cubes are filled with mostly short-stemmed flowers (a feature that promotes their longevity). The horizontal line created by the cubes is reinforced with materials that float above the flowers in a sheltering fashion. Sometimes you may have fresh materials, like equisetum or flax leaves, that work well to create these lines. If you don't, you can find creative substitutions that serve the same function.

Colorful, bendable plastic straws offer one option for a light, fun version of the design contemplated in the template sketch. Green button mums are positioned at various heights, which brings a botanical element up into the superstructure with the straws. The small button mums also add depth to the design, but most of the flowers, and all of the larger ones, are kept below the straws, creating an effect of two separate tiers or dimensions. Orange and yellow spray roses harmonize with the colors of the straws; white daisies add to the playful mood, while dendrobium orchids extend the horizontal line at the rim of the cubes.

## DESIGN TIP

Plastic drinking straws with built-in angles can be inserted one into another.

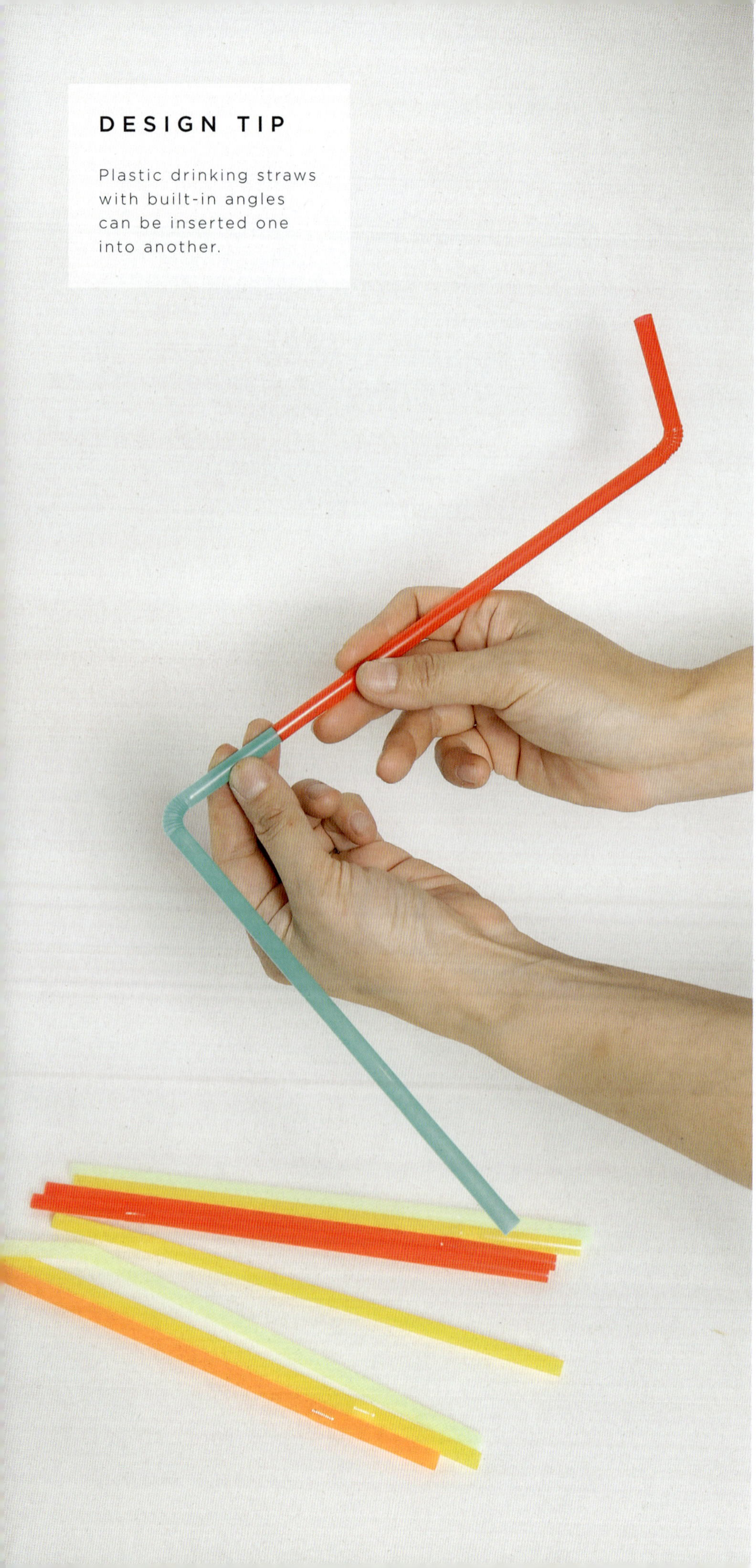

Sturdy and wide, variegated flax leaves serve beautifully to establish horizontal line. A primary leaf can be stabilized in position by inserting the tip through a slit cut in another leaf. Here, two lengths of flat copper wire reinforce the primary line, seeming to float above and below the flax, but likewise stabilized with slits cut in the flax leaves and in the wire itself. Together, all of these angled materials form a sturdy superstructure that shelters a colorful basing with a clearly defined focal area.

Diagonal lines, established with the flax leaves but also with liatris and with 'Xanadu' philodendron leaves, lend dynamic energy to the design. They are echoed in star shapes made with narrow flat copper wire, accents that bring unity to the design along with creative flair. Some of the star points are accented with petals of gerbera daisies, in the same color as those in the focal area. Likewise, rows of gerbera petals are glued to the ends of the horizontal strips of wide flat wire. Flame-like, they make the entire design look like it is racing toward the left.

Midollino sticks are colorful, slender, and flexible, which allows you to create more elegant, curvy lines, some almost perfectly horizontal, others bent at dynamic angles. Using the midollino in small bundles banded with bullion wire strengthens the line. Tailored Italian ruscus is woven through the midollino, lending additional movement and a natural feel. The focal area is created with two red anthuriums inserted as tiers, sheltering the green cymbidiums underneath. On the other side, 'Freedom' roses are tucked in low to anchor the visual weight of the design.

Here the horizontal lines are created with equisetum and mahogany bamboo. Some of the lines are almost perfectly horizontal, but others are set diagonally off-kilter, which gives the design energy and keeps it from becoming too static. Orange lilies and spray roses are arranged together with green cymbidium orchids to create an area of focal emphasis. Floral foam is covered with river pebbles to add natural interest to the design while keeping the negative space created by the horizontal lines above clean and transparent.

# **CURVILINEAR** DESIGN

More often than not, flower and plant stems are fundamentally straight. Any time that you can incorporate curving or even wavy lines to a design, you are adding that little bit of dynamic energy that leads the eye playfully through the design. Why not have a go at creating some designs that are actually dominated by curving, weaving lines?

Oasis Floral Mesh offers a simple and creative way to introduce curvy lines to a design, here reinforced with Oasis wide flat wire. The mesh also serves as a grid to control stem insertions, which is necessary in this case because the design is created in a clear glass cube without foam. Together, the silver mesh and wire bring a metallic, industrial feel to the design, in pleasing contrast to the sunny colors and informal placement of the flowers, which are quite varied in form and texture. The monochromatic color scheme brings all of these contrasts to the fore.

## DESIGN TIP

Oasis Floral Mesh is easily trimmed and formed to any desired shape.

# **TRIANGLE** DESIGN

Try playing with an open, L-shaped structure as a way of creating asymmetric formal linear designs that offer maximum impact with minimal materials. Such designs typically offer a certain height and width, but they must be carefully composed to achieve good visual balance, with a strong emphasis in the focal area.

A stem topped with two lily buds but trimmed of all foliage here establishes a slender vertical line. Because it is slightly diagonal, bending off the axis, it adds a pleasing tension to the composition. The line of the stem continues with the red roses in the focal area and dark green anthurium foliage below.

Variegated aspidistra leaves define the horizontal line. The aspidistra leaves are inserted with a shadowing technique. There is space between them, and the parallel curves look natural, but they are carefully controlled with wire, which is placed between two aspidistra leaves that have been glued back-to-back (see page 31).

The focal area is strongly established with red roses and accented with rolled variegated anthurium leaves on one side, tight white lily buds on the other. Baby 'Xanadu' philodendron foliage counterbalances the aspidistra leaves on the other side. Finally, silver flat wire, fashioned into leaf shapes, pulls the silver tone of the cylinder vase up among the flowers and leaves, lending unity to the composition.

## DESIGN TIP

Pinch flat wire lightly with needle-nose pliers to create neat, shapely leaf tips.

CHAPTER 5

# Wedding Design



Wedding design is a popular category, nearly always included in any floral-design competition or evaluation session. Usually, the assignment is to create a bouquet (flowers to wear being a separate category, covered in the next chapter). Further requirements may be specified as to the nature and style of the bouquet, just as they are when you meet with a bride—and of course, you can only use the flowers you are given.

What remains consistent is that, working within the constraints of well-executed bouquet mechanics, you must address all the scoring criteria that apply to any other example of formal linear design, including line, depth, balance, focal area, color harmony, and of course, creative flair.

# CASCADING BRIDAL BOUQUET

To create a bridal bouquet with a cascade presents certain challenges, both technical and artistic—which is precisely why this type of bouquet gives you as a floral designer an opportunity to show how good you are. It requires a cascading line that falls down and juts a little forward from the center of the bouquet.

A cascade can be built into a bridal bouquet based on almost any type of mechanic—including, as you will see later in this chapter, hand-tied bouquets. First, however, we have three cascading bouquets made in medium-size, straight-handle Wedding Belle holders. In each case, the handle is finished with foliage (the first step in making the design).

Where a cascading line is prominently featured, it should always be counterbalanced with design elements on the opposite side of the bouquet (the top). These must be shorter than the cascade but should have a similar visual weight. The greatest visual weight, however, should always be given to the area of focal emphasis—which can be accented with a variety of design techniques.

If you are lacking botanical materials with a natural extension and drape, you can still create a cascading effect with design accessories such as midollino. Here, the visual weight of the slender midollino is enhanced by gathering the sticks together into groups and banding them with bullion wire. The bullion wire also allows bending of the midollino into shapes resembling tails of wide ribbon. The cascade is then balanced with smaller accents of midollino on the other side. Green cymbidiums dominate the focal area; they are a key element in the bouquet's green and white color harmony.

Red anthuriums, backed with a large philodendron leaf, give this bouquet a bold and dramatic look. The forward dimension of the jutting, downward-pointing philodendron leaf is reinforced with curls of lily grass, banded here and there with red bullion, which reinforces the color harmony. The joining and banding also gives the lily grass added weight and substance, so it doesn't fly up. Blades of grass can also be inserted through tiny slits in other blades of grass as a way of stabilizing the shape of the cascade.

Bent equisetum is used to balance both the cascade and the visual weight of the red anthuriums that anchor the focal area. White and light green materials occupy the upper part of the focal area: lily buds are inserted together in a tight grouping, along with 'Green Ball' dianthus and mini green hydrangea, plus a green cymbidium bloom that serves to harmonize the red and green halves of the bouquet. The bottom of the bouquet holder and the handle are both covered with green leaves.

In this bouquet, white dendrobium orchids are used to create the cascading line, which is balanced with a layered pair of anthurium leaves on the other side. 'Freedom' roses occupy the focal area, reinforced by overshadowing loops of lily grass. Hypericum berries and groupings of white freesia and of button mums are tucked next to the red roses, adding interest and texture to the focal.

Judges evaluating any bridal bouquet will look critically at the underside of the bouquet and at the handle, in terms of both aesthetics and mechanics. As they should! To a bride, the appearance, security and comfort of the handle are not mere "details" but of paramount importance to her experience and impression of your professionalism. Working with a holder, always cover the handle and the underside before you do anything else. Here, variegated aspidistra and criss-crossing bands of lily grass give the underside of the bouquet a nice finish.

**The Usefulness of Accent Materials**
One of the difficulties when creating any hand-held bouquet is to give it line value, depth and dimension along with a recognizable form. Without all of these qualities, your bouquet will not get enough points to score well in evaluation or competition. Decorative wire, or a similar accent material like flat cane, can be a useful tool for meeting this challenge. Bridal customers may also appreciate the cost-effectiveness of wire or cane accents as a way of extending the size and impact of the bouquet, without adding more flowers.

This bouquet is simply a compact, round ball of flowers in a bouquet holder, enhanced with an open wire structure that adds line, motion and depth while it echoes and reinforces the classic, spherical form of the flower cluster. The wire structure can and should be assembled in advance, using sections of flat wire (here in copper color) with the ends curled under. The sections are glued together to form an empty cup that embraces the bouquet and leads the eye back in towards the center.

With any bouquet in a bouquet holder, it's important to take care of covering the handle perfectly, even before you start to work on the flowers. If you don't do this before you start designing, you will soon find yourself in trouble. Here, croton leaves are glued to the bottom side of the bouquet holder as well as to the handle. The patterns of the croton leaves pick up the flower colors, contributing to the bouquet's unified color harmony.

## DESIGN TIP

Trim foliage to fit the underside of a bouquet holder before securing it with floral adhesive.

Here, a cascading line is built with a few strips of flat cane. A similar effect could be achieved with flat wire or with blades or strips of foliage. To add a rustic feel, silver-toned tape, printed with a birch bark pattern, was adhered to the cane. Some of the flat cane is used full width; some of it is split to make thinner strips. A thin strip can be inserted through a slit in a wider strip of cane to stabilize the structure.

The cascade not only adds line movement and depth to this bouquet, but it also strengthens the focal area, framing the two 'Free Spirit' roses and the cymbidium orchids within strong contrasting lines. The color and custom texture of the flat cane makes this bouquet stand out for creative flair.

A single large, distinctive bloom—like the anthurium featured here—can be the key to a winning bouquet. If you have such a flower, begin your creative process by thinking how to show it to best advantage. Then fill in with other flowers to make that bloom stand out.

Here, the anthurium is backed by a single monstera leaf in a similar shape, and that distinctive shape is echoed with accent materials: wire accents and knotted loops of variegated lily grass. The repetition of the leaf shape adds rhythm and depth to the composition. The fuchsia color of the wire shapes connects them visually with the roses, tulips, and stock.

Again, with a bouquet created in a holder that has a plastic handle, it's important to begin by covering the handle, which is done here by wrapping it with faux aspidistra ribbon.

# **HANDTIED** BOUQUETS

Popular with some brides, a handtied bouquet may also be a requirement in the wedding-design category for a competition or evaluation. You may also be asked to design a bouquet but not provided with a bouquet holder. It's important to have ideas and techniques up your sleeve for creating a handtied bouquet that meets all the criteria applied to formal linear design. When you do, the handtied method might even save you some time, since you won't need to prep the holder or cover your mechanics.

This bouquet begins with an old trick: carnation heads (still attached to their stems) are skewered onto a length of aluminum wire. The wire is then bent into a circular shape. The open carnation ring serves as a kind of armature that supports the addition of other flowers. With these you can establish a strong focal area and add line movement to the basic round shape. Here, all of that is achieved with green cymbidium orchids on wire stems, white callas, Italian ruscus, myrtle, a mini monstera leaf, and variegated lily grass.

## DESIGN TIP

Snip aluminum wire at an angle to make a sharp point and simply push it through carnation calyxes to create an encircling armature for a handtied bouquet.

With a handtied, as with a bridal bouquet in a holder, wire accents can be a useful tool for adding line and depth along with creative flair. It's important, however, not to let these accents appear as an afterthought; they must be creatively integrated into the bouquet. Wire accents will draw the attention of the judges, so they must be purposeful, not random.

Here, aluminum wire in a fuchsia color is bent into angled shapes that duplicate the shapes of the aspidistra leaves below them, pointing in the same direction. Some of the wire shapes are enhanced with bullion wire, to give them more substance and dimension. The wire shapes do what the aspidistra leaves alone could not: they create a powerful, dynamic cascade, strengthen the color scheme, and add an unmistakable creative touch to the bouquet.

A round shape is the natural tendency of the handtied format. Here, green hypericum berries on long wire stems add a burst of energy to the simple round shape. Combining the long wire stems into angled pairs (as seen in the how-to photo), rather than adding them in as single stems, gives more control over their positioning.

Within the bouquet itself, flowers are grouped rather than mixed up, for added color impact. A large aralia leaf and curving heads of millet spring out from among the round shapes of the other flowers. On the underside, a row of carnations gives the bouquet a clean, decorative finish, along with a grass tie.

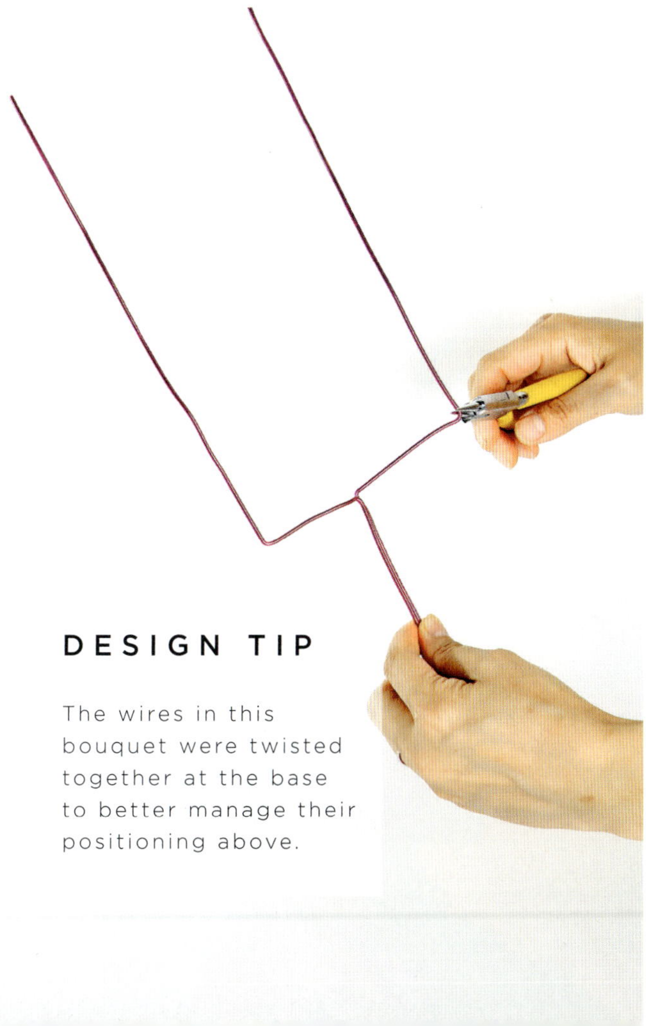

## DESIGN TIP

The wires in this bouquet were twisted together at the base to better manage their positioning above.

Another way to give your handtied bouquet interest is to create a simple and quick armature with the material given to you. Here's one idea: carnation stems, tied into a star shape. You can add as many stem sections as you need to create a design grid that supports stems inserted through it to make a handtied bouquet. In the finished design, you have two separate layers and fun lines that draw the eye in toward the focal area, created here with big bright sunflowers.

## DESIGN TIP

A quick and easy armature can be fashioned with carnation stems, secured with Bind Wire.

CHAPTER 6

# Flowers to Wear

In commercial floristry, the wearable designs that you create for weddings or prom may be relatively small in size, but they always draw lots of notice and attention. Therefore, you always want this type of work to be the best that you can do.

Similarly, in a surprise-package situation—whether it's a floral design competition or a professional evaluation—the flowers-to-wear category is one of the most important. Why? Because, even though your finished design may not have the large visual impact of a showy bouquet or sympathy design, it counts equally with all your other designs in your overall score. With planning and practice, you can create a wrist or shoulder corsage, hair ornament or body jewelry design that meets all of the scoring criteria and do it very quickly. Yet it will earn you just as many points as your work in other, more time-consuming categories.

Remember that the judging criteria are the same as with any other design. Your design must have line value, focal emphasis and depth and be well balanced visually as well as physically, along with demonstrating good mechanics, color harmony, and everything else.

Flowers-to-wear designs do require some special techniques and strategies. This, therefore, is a category where it pays to have prepared lots of sketches and to have honed your skills with wire and with cold glue.

You don't know exactly what materials will be made available to you. But in most tests and competitions, you can expect to receive at least a bag of 12-gauge decorative aluminum wire, a spool of bullion wire, and a tube of floral adhesive.

The key to a successful wearable design is to begin with a simple geometric shape. You probably want to avoid making complicated, delicate, swirling patterns with your wire. Your work with wire should be very clean and precise. It should even look "machine-made"—as different as possible from a child's craft project. If you make your wire into swirls, for example, it's better to fashion them into tightly wound coils with little or no space between the coils. On the other hand, if you decide to shape your wire into random swirls, make sure the look is clearly random and free of any pattern. Your intentions must be clear.

Practice your skills with cold glue (floral adhesive), so that your materials adhere securely to the base and no residue shows after the glue has dried. Make sure your gluing surface is coarse (rough it up a little if necessary): cold glue can easily pop off of highly polished, smooth surfaces. Apply the glue to both of the surfaces that you are gluing together, but don't use excessive glue.

Once you are adept and comfortable with using cold glue and with using wire to create a variety of bases and accents, you can quickly create wearable designs that will earn high scores from judges and customers alike.

# WRIST CORSAGE

A bangle made with flat wire has become a classic and adaptable foundation for a wrist corsage. Here we have three wrist corsages that all rely on this same foundation, but with very different results in terms of style.

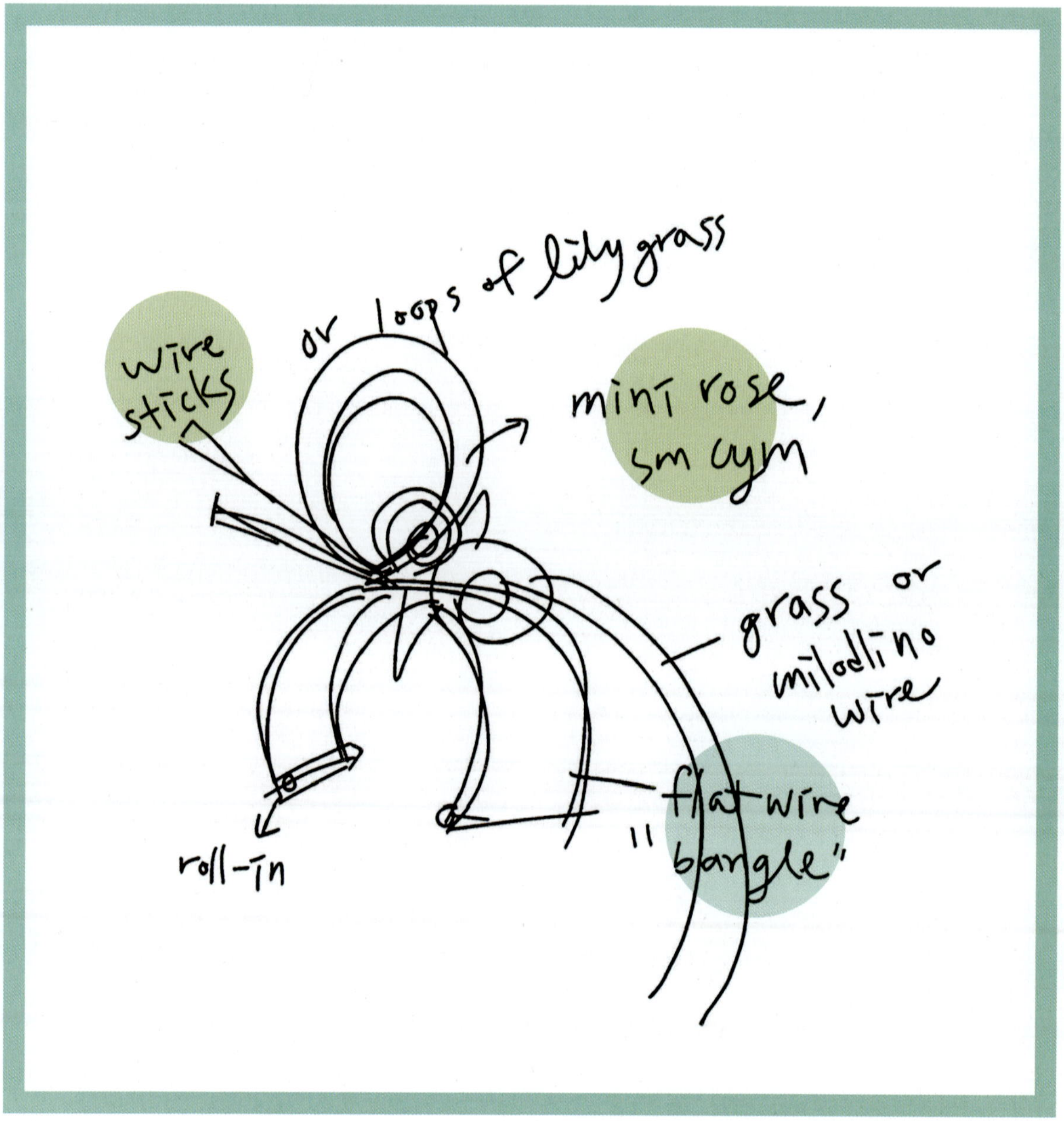




Remember that your template sketch serves as a springboard for your creativity. You create the sketch using materials you have at hand. Later, you will likely need to make substitutions, but the sketch serves as a reminder of the most important elements. Here, it suggests how layering of materials in the focal area can add depth to the design, while the addition of materials that extend beyond the focal area create line movement that leads the eye out and back in again to the focal.

Taking inspiration from the spreading petals of a dendrobium orchid, which serves as the focal flower, wire petals were added as creative accents that bring line value into the picture, along with a more extended effect of layering for added depth. Diamond Wire was shaped into the outline of petals; the larger outlines were then filled with dusty miller foliage, cut to fit each leaf shape. The dusty miller adds an element of texture and artistry without taking away from the strong lines created by the wire shapes. The leaf shapes, along with pointy rosebuds, ruscus, and equisetum, all add layered depth to the design along with gently curving, extended radial lines.

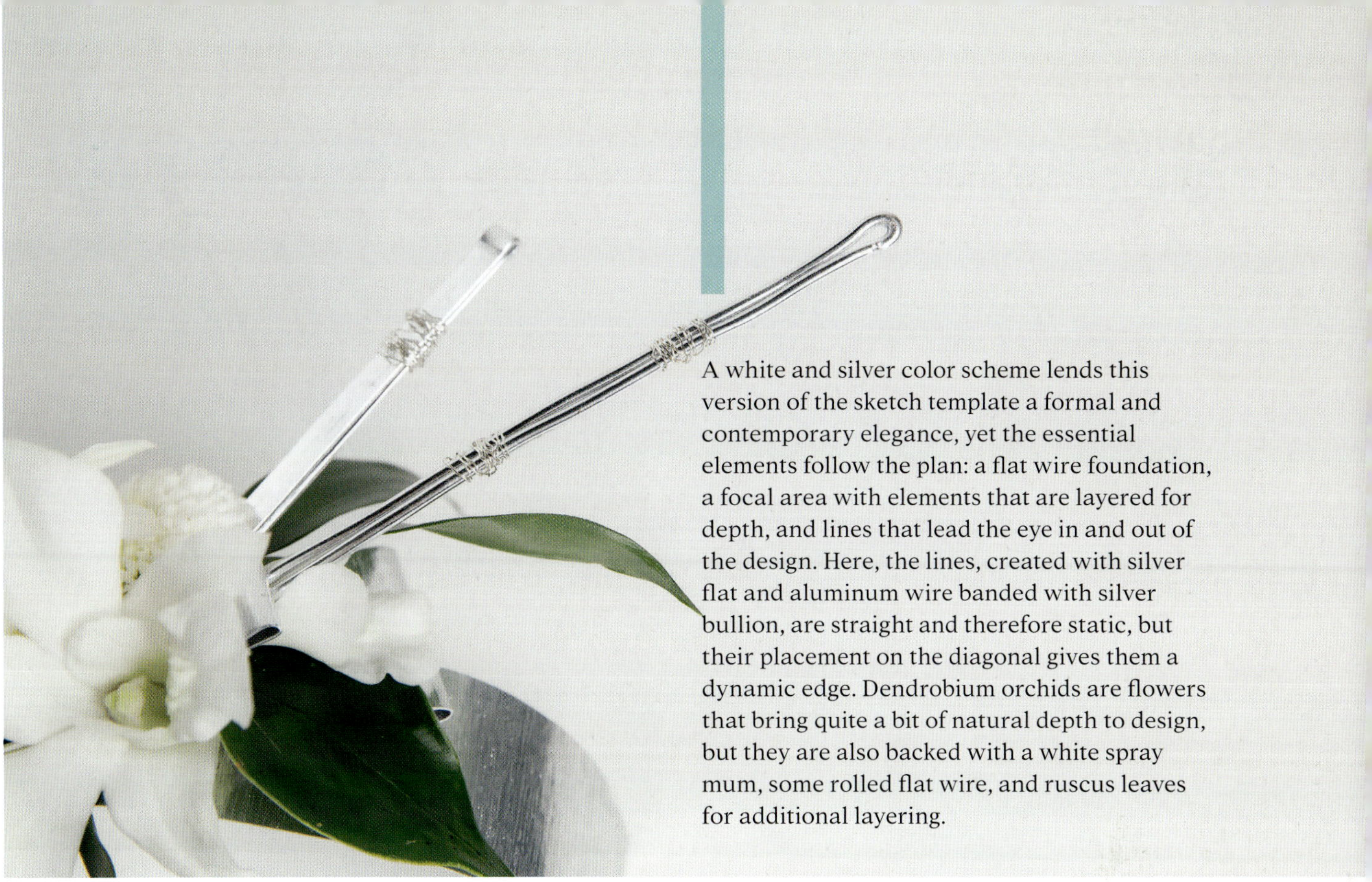

A white and silver color scheme lends this version of the sketch template a formal and contemporary elegance, yet the essential elements follow the plan: a flat wire foundation, a focal area with elements that are layered for depth, and lines that lead the eye in and out of the design. Here, the lines, created with silver flat and aluminum wire banded with silver bullion, are straight and therefore static, but their placement on the diagonal gives them a dynamic edge. Dendrobium orchids are flowers that bring quite a bit of natural depth to design, but they are also backed with a white spray mum, some rolled flat wire, and ruscus leaves for additional layering.

## DESIGN TIP

Using flat wire for wearable designs, always roll the cut ends, tucking away sharp edges.

For color harmony, this design combines a 'Yellow Babe' spray rose and rosebud with wide gold flat wire and gold etched wire. The etched wire is fashioned into swirled medallions that imitate the round shape of the rose. Placed just underneath the rose, they provide a decorative background that lends depth to the design. Twin loops of lily grass add to the layered effect and to the visual rhythm that is created through repetition of a pattern. Meanwhile, snipped blades and long tips of lily grass provide flowing line.

# BOUTONNIERE

When does a floral designer create something smaller than a boutonniere? Almost never! Which makes it all the more impressive when you meet the challenge of designing a boutonniere that demonstrates everything you know and can employ about the principles and elements that govern sophisticated, artistic floral design.

Starting with a strong geometric shape is always a good strategy. Here, the verticals and horizontals in the rectangular foundation are emphasized by constructing the rectangle out of cardboard as an open window frame and covering it with artificial variegated aspidistra leaf. Dynamic diagonal lines are added with two tiny reed sticks, reminiscent of chopsticks. A single fuchsia dendrobium orchid bloom establishes the focal area clearly and simply. Nonetheless, the focal point is further emphasized with fuchsia-colored aluminum wire, shaped into floral petals, as if they were extra orchid petals. The wire accents add dimension and depth—one of the most difficult elements to achieve in a boutonniere. The color and texture of these accents is repeated on the reeds with bands of bullion wire.

## DESIGN TIP

Striped artificial foliage playfully reinforces the verticals and horizontals in this foundation.

Coins made with coiled aluminum wire offer another idea for a boutonniere foundation with strong geometry. When you use aluminum wire to create a round medallion, make sure the coil is tight, not loose, with as few gaps as possible, for a clean finished shape. Here, silver coins are added to a gold base at different levels, to create depth; one coil of silver wire hovers directly above the focal area.

In scale with the small size of a boutonniere, the variegation in colorful croton leaves can be a way to add dynamic lines on top of a rectangular cardboard base. The leaves are glued to the base with cold glue, then wrapped with bullion wire. At the focal point, round materials (a green button mum, accented with two hypericum berries) provide a resting point for the eye, while petals clipped from a birds of paradise bloom and an orange gerbera daisy elongate the lines in the croton foliage.

### DESIGN TIP

As a foundation cover, croton foliage brings both color and line.

# NECKLACE

Lately, we've seen lots of "floral fashion" designs in magazines and on social media. As the floral necklace has received more media exposure, it has become a requirement in more floral design competitions. To do well in this category, you need a quite specific blueprint: first because a necklace can be a very time-consuming project, and second because it can be tricky to achieve the high scores in all of the judging criteria, just by the nature of this type of design.

Specifically, for a test or competition, your best bet is to go with a choker or similarly short and tight necklace versus any other style, such as a chain or a long necklace with a pendant. A necklace in the choker style can be done quickly. It offers a clear, definite form in the foundation. Keep the part around sides and back of the neck sturdy and simple. Adding too many decorative elements just here can distract from your focal area and create confusing lines.

Working with a simple neckline, and keeping in mind that you want to aim for perfect scores in each of the design criteria (focal area, depth, scale, color harmony, and so on), you may want to pay special attention to creative line movement. Make sure your lines have impact and rhythm. Create a strong focal area. It can be in a pendant style that is simple in itself but embellished with additional creative techniques. Take care that your finished design has depth. It is all too easy to create a necklace that is completely flat. Depth and texture are the keys to success in this category!

## DESIGN TIP

These coiled medallions are attached to each other with bullion wire, not glue, so they will dangle.

Echoing the form of the choker itself, a simple round circle made with gold Diamond Wire, this necklace features medallions in various sizes made by coiling the same wire into coin-shaped disks. The medallions are connected to each other in various ways with bullion wire: sometimes adjacent, sometimes overlapping to create depth. They are not cemented together but dangle as a group. A single white daisy is glued to the center medallion; smaller white and yellow blooms and petals are added elsewhere to the foundation. The flowers repeat the round shape and color values of the swirling medallions. A few strands of thin gold jeweler's wire and bullion wire are draped over the daisy to add some dynamic line and additional depth. It all adds up to a design with a feeling of casual innocence.

The foundation here is quick and easy to make, with a long flat panel constructed separately and added to the neckline structure, all made with blue aluminum wire. The neckline is reinforced with strands of lily grass and with thin blue wire strung with a few hypericum berries. The pendant panel is simple yet impactful in its slim shape and stripey lines. A focal point is created by gluing a green mini cymbidium bloom to the foundation, along with part of a thistle, green button mums and green hypericum berries. Two blue delphinium florets add some lightness to the composition and provide additional resting places for the eye.

Wavy lines can be acceptable as an alternative to straight lines or perfect curves, as long as you use them consistently, so that your intentions are very clear. Here, shorter lengths of curvy wire have been added to the main neckline using glue and bullion wire, to give the finished shape body and rhythm. A dendrobium orchid blossom is augmented with just part of another one, along with gomphrena blooms, to give the focal area and accent flowers just the right scale and dimension.

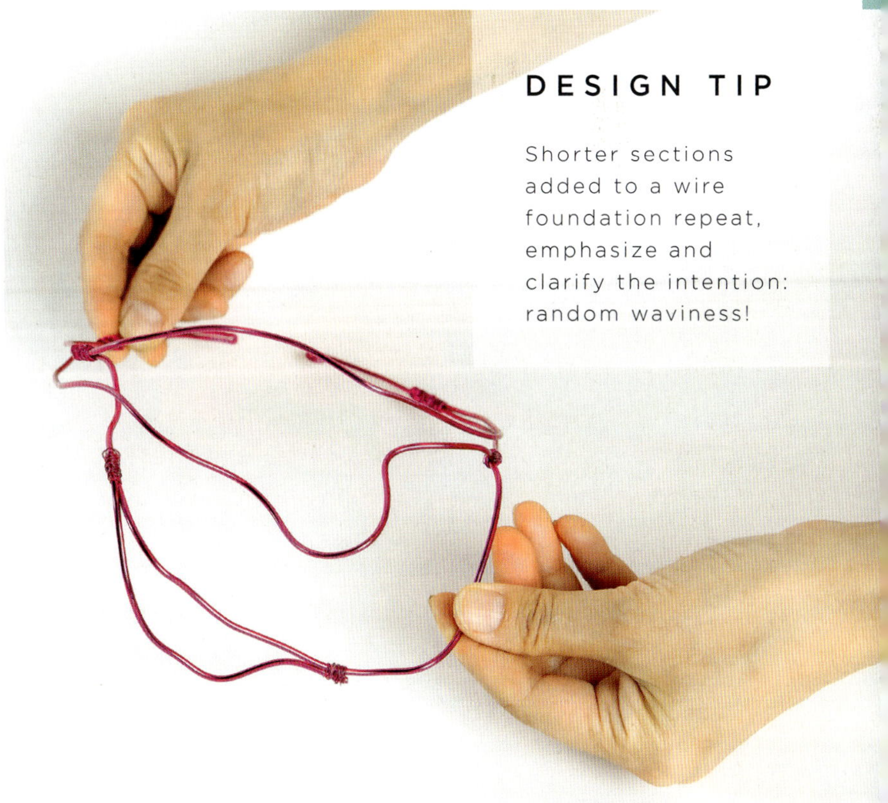

## DESIGN TIP

Shorter sections added to a wire foundation repeat, emphasize and clarify the intention: random waviness!

# HAIR PIECE

The same guidelines apply to hair pieces as to necklaces. The important thing to remember is that to be practical, a hairpiece requires a very sturdy foundation. Style choices include crown, haloes, headbands, and combs.

A doubled length of flat wire makes a sturdy headband for this hair piece. A small piece of cardboard provides the gluing surface needed to add a cluster of floral materials including variegated croton leaves. More flat wire swirls over the focal area, adding dynamic line value.

## DESIGN TIP

A double length of flat wire makes for slender tips and a wide center, with cardboard added for a gluing surface.

CHAPTER 7

# Sympathy Design



The Sympathy Design category may include any design that is appropriate for a funeral or celebration of life, such as a casket spray, standing spray, memorial design or cremation urn. You need to be careful to plan this category, as most of sympathy designs require more time and products to create. As you plan your sympathy design, set all the materials aside that you are planning to use for this piece, so that you will not find yourself short of flowers or foliage.

Perhaps the one most important thing to remember in this category is to completely cover your mechanics as the very first step. The foundation materials that will likely be provided—such as a large foam cage, wire easel, casket saddle, or wreath base—offer a large surface to cover, and it becomes extremely difficult to cover your mechanics perfectly once you have started adding flowers. Therefore, make sure you take care of hiding your mechanics before you make any stem insertions. Otherwise, you will end up with all sorts of trouble affecting your time management and overall design.

# STANDING **EASEL** DESIGN

At some point, every floral designer needs to know how to create a standing easel design that will serve the expressive needs of a memorial or funeral service with beauty, elegance, and dramatic impact. For good reason, this type of design is also a standard component in floral design competitions and in the in-person evaluation for professional credentials. With its ample size and front-facing orientation, it offers you an ideal opportunity to establish a strong focal point, articulate dramatic line, and take advantage of all the creative power behind the principles and elements of design, while at the same time you showcase your mastery of various techniques of embellishment.

The examples in this book rely on a foam cage secured to the easel, which gives you plenty of space for insertions and offers a good opportunity to showcase creative techniques in the focal area. In a surprise-package situation, you may also be given a floral-foam cross. However, it will be up to you whether to use the cross or not. If you choose to make a cross and you have other materials that you can use to create that shape, you may be better off using those other materials, because the foam cross will contain your design within a given look already. You can create your own cross shape by bundling dried birch branches, by tying sections of rivercane together, by using flax or any long, stiff foliage as your base.

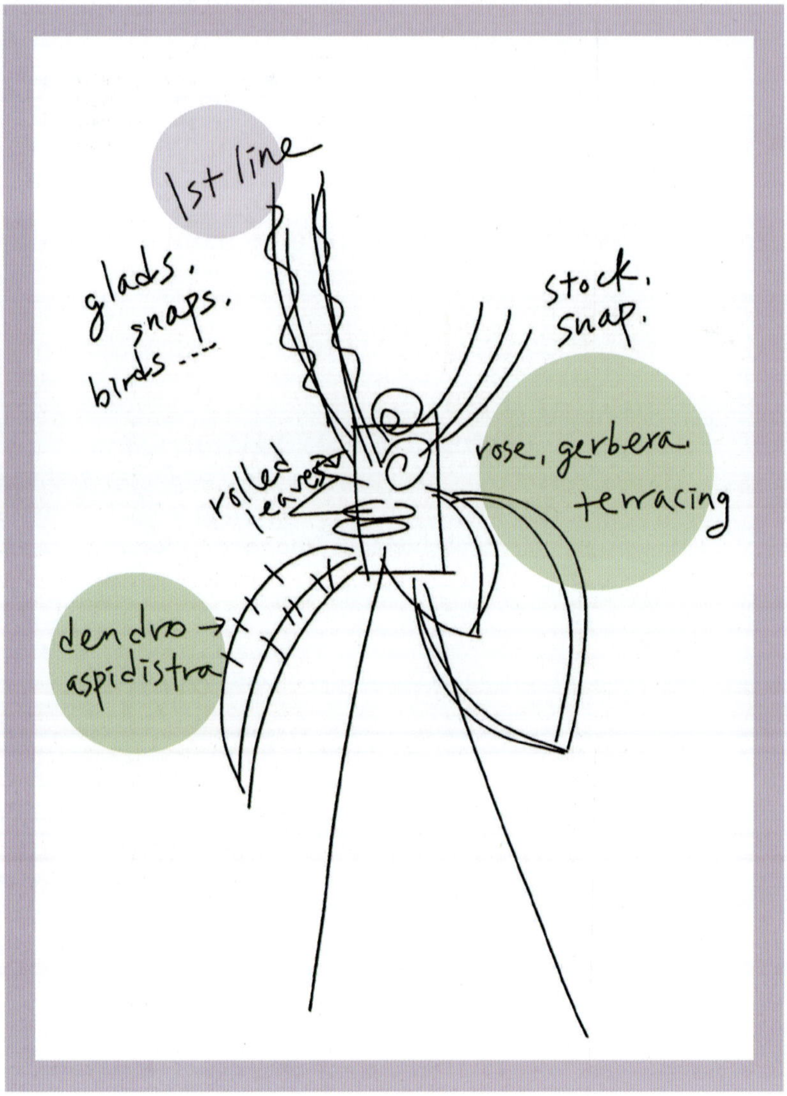


The template sketch shows a simple, asymmetrical design in the formal linear style, with an X shape that brings emphasis to the focal area where the two lines meet. The lines that form the X are quite obvious, so if you are following a sketch like this one, you would want to make sure you do something extra to add creative flair to these lines.

Where you have crossing lines that strongly emphasize the focal area, it's important to choose, as your main focal flowers, blooms with substantial visual weight, like these large white Oriental lilies. The crossing lines themselves then give an opportunity to showcase line flowers like liatris and gladiolus.

Here, the primary line (meaning, the one that is longer at the top of the design) starts on the left, comprising liatris stems in staggered lengths, reinforced with lavender chrysanthemums. The secondary line is defined with iris. A typical form flower, iris is best seen in profile, with space around the flower heads. Loops of lily grass add depth and interest to the iris stems at top right, without distracting from their distinctive shapes. The loops are tied with bands of purple flat wire.

Below the focal area, the secondary line continues on the opposite side with more iris, reinforced with gladiolus and snapdragons, which provide the visual weight needed here for balance (to keep the design from looking top-heavy). The primary line continues on the bottom right with ribbons of woven lily grass. Of course, in a limited-time situation like a competition, you would only use a technique like this if you have practiced it and know that you can complete the weaving quickly.

The design is anchored with large dark foliages (philodendron and aralia leaves). Foliages like these can lend visual impact (with light-colored flowers outlined against them) and have a unifying effect, but normally they need to be balanced with smaller leaves and more detailed elements.

All the blooms and leaves are in white or in tints and tones of lavender and purple, plus green. The result is an analogous color harmony (green being a neutral color in floral design).

At first glance, this design might look as though it has strayed a long way from the template sketch. But the X shape is still there, and the sketch still provides guidance for a well-balanced design, with adjustments made along the way. The primary line on the left is established with birds of paradise; it is extended and balanced on the opposite bottom side with layered, extra-large monstera leaves. The spine of the upper monstera leaf directly continues the line of the lower birds of paradise stem. The secondary line begins on top with orange snapdragons, paired with accents of angled equisetum, placed so as to offset the wide surface area of the monstera leaves below. The line continues on the bottom left with purple dendrobium orchids.

In the focal area, the equisetum triangles are duplicated with orange flat wire, bringing greater unity to the composition through repetition of form. Orange gerberas and 'Free Spirit' roses make a strong statement as focal flowers, supported by rolled aspidistra leaves. The rolled and layered foliage, in particular, lends great depth to this design.

Here, the simple, diagonal lines of the template sketch are strongly established with red ginger on one side, set against a backdrop of birds of paradise foliage, and anthuriums on the other. The primary diagonal line continues below with red carnations set against more birds of paradise leaves. By contrast, the anthuriums, with no foliage backdrop, seem to float in space. They require, for visual balance, the two strands of braided lily grass on the opposite side. The secondary line continues below with variegated foliage and white dendrobium orchids.

A grouping of 'Freedom' roses at the focal area might have seemed too simple, even clichéd, without the addition of folded and layered foliage (anthurium, aspidistra, and aralia), plus braided loops of lily grass. These various shapes add depth and texture to the design.

Sympathy Design

This design strays quite far from the template sketch, but the underlying idea of crossing lines that emphasize the focal area is still there. At the top of the design, curly willow tips emerge on each side from the focal area (defined by large white lilies) and are tied together in the center, creating an arch that frames the yellow roses. Below the focal area, we can still see lines that form the bottom of an X. In this design, a central axis is also clearly but delicately defined, with craspedia stems above and the spine of a palm frond below.

Something like a contemporary cross is represented here with strong horizontal and vertical lines. A bold, dynamic, barely diagonal line is set against these horizontals and verticals, crossing behind them at the point where they intersect, further emphasizing the focal point. The focal area sits just above the center of the cross, where an orange gerbera faces fully forward, its visual weight reinforced by orange carnations behind it and by a large medallion of coiled wire just below. The large monstera leaf is crucial to the visual balance of this design: it anchors the design's very tall and long extensions above and below (namely, birds of paradise blooms and leaves, more orange gerberas in a line, and a linear stem of gladiolus like a flashing tail). Blunt-cut flax leaves reinforce the horizontal arm of the cross with their variegated lines as well as with their positioning. Placed in parallel with the pale, neutral rivercane, they serve to integrate the rivercane with the other fresh materials in the design.

# SYMPATHY **WREATH** DESIGN

Very often, in testing and competition, you will be provided with a round wreath base filled with floral foam. Since you will be working with limited time and material, it makes sense to begin by covering the wreath base with a given material such as aspidistra. You can still make insertions through the aspidistra or other foliage, but you won't need to cover the wreath base with many smaller insertions. With this strategy, you have gained time; you take advantage of the strong geometric shape in the wreath form; and it will be easier to create a line movement and a strong focal area, without obscuring the round outline of the wreath.

A simple way to preserve the impression made by a round wreath form is to let flowers spill in radial lines from a well-defined focal area at the base of the wreath. Here, clean primary and secondary lines also rise up from the flowers at the base in parallel fashion. These integrate the flowers with the wreath form and keep the composition well balanced. The focal point (a white lily, backed with a second white lily for a feeling of depth) is placed directly between the two vertical lines.

A strong diagonal superimposed on the round wreath form is another way of energizing your design. Here, foliage establishes the diagonal, with striped hala leaves in the middle, ginger leaves at top and bottom. Clusters of flowers give the eye resting points at the two places where the diagonal intersects the circle. Of the two, however, the lower cluster of flowers, together with the ginger leaves that extend from it, is clearly the focal area. Its size and visual weight establish its dominance. Decorative gold wire orbits around both clusters, adding depth, movement, and texture contrast.

For a softer line, flowers and foliage can be placed so as to duplicate the round shape of the ring base. The tailored Italian ruscus sprouts branchlets that reinforce the circle with a delicate corolla; white callas follow the circle's curve but stand out against it. The focal area is created at the bottom with a white gerbera daisy, 'Green Tea' roses, and green cymbidiums, accented with rolled leaves, millet, and hypericum berries. A counterpoint is created on top of the wreath with materials that are set close to the wreath surface and to each other, as in pavé technique. Even so, they offer contrasts in height that give depth to the design: mini roses, equisetum, green dianthus and hydrangea. An asymmetric tail of white dendrobium and lily grass leads the eye away from the circle and back inward in a harmonious curve.

# SYMPATHY **CASKET TOP**

Creating a casket-top design is no small task. It takes a lot of flowers and foliage as well as a lot of time. You have wider leeway, however, in your choice of flowers and foliage than is the case with wedding bouquets or with flowers to wear. In the latter categories, only certain materials will be appropriate to your design. Therefore, in a surprise-package situation, the best strategy is to set materials aside for wedding designs and flowers to wear before you start working on your sympathy casket.

As always, whatever you think customers may find acceptable in commercial design, when your casket spray will be judged by professionals, you must be sure to employ the artistic power of all the principles and elements of design. Indeed, if you take similar care with your commercial sympathy work, you may be surprised to discover what a positive response it draws from customers.

A low, spreading shape might seem natural to a casket-top design—and it is!—but the composition gains interest and energy with the strategy that we have relied on for many other types of design as well: an X shape with lines that meet in the center, drawing attention to the focal area. Here, angular lines are created with folded and woven hala leaves. They are duplicated with wired stems of equisetum, bent into right angles and connected at the top. The angled lines created by these rectangles are reinforced with snapdragons; they continue through the focal area to the other side, where the lines emerge in stems of white gladiolus. The other line that forms an X is done with yellow roses, which define an implied line, leading into the focal area and continuing on the other side with white carnations. Yellow lilies and large white chrysanthemums claim the focal area, accented with loops of variegated lily grass.

An L shape can also be an effective strategy for a casket spray with dramatic interest. Here, a double layer of variegated ginger leaves serves as a backdrop for the strongly elaborated focal area. The rolled tips of the ginger leaves seem to bow in the direction of a powerful red zone, blooming with the different shapes and textures of roses, carnations, and anthuriums. Within the monochromatic zone, these differences in shape and texture become more noticeable. Loops of red flat wire further draw attention to the focal area. Purple flowers on either side give the design its necessary breadth and extension. A variety of foliages is used on the front of the design to add depth and rhythm.

# **CREMATION URN** FLOWERS

For this category of design in testing or competition, you probably would be given a round or square wreath base. As in the sympathy wreath category, your best strategy is not to fill the entire ring or square base with flowers. Remember that you have limited time and materials. Start by completely covering the base with foliage. You have a powerful beginning with a simple geometric shape. On top of this foundation, you will need to create a focal area and other elements that stand out distinctly from the base.

The process for an urn design similar to this one is to wrap the round ring base with aspidistra leaves first, then start designing with attention to opposite points at the front and back of the ring. At the back, create a backdrop, as here with budded gladiolus and carnations, supported by a few liatris stems. At the front, fully opened blooms taken from the lowest part of the gladiolus stems are positioned in the focal area, along with white roses and lavender carnations.

The two points, back and front, are then connected with circles of green midollino, following the contour of the ring base, and with lily grass. On one side, white callas reinforce the circle; on the other, tailored palm leaf creates a playful rhythm.

The color combination of lavender and white is so simple and clean, it invites the addition of textured details, like the raft made with leftover carnation stems, skewered together into a flat panel and positioned next to the focal area.

This green and white design for a cremation urn could have been made from the same template sketch, but it emerges with a very different result. As before, it relies on a low focal point in front and a wide, tall backdrop at the back. A pair of ginger leaves swiftly establishes the backdrop, with sentry posts on either side. In the focal area, 'Green Tea' roses and 'Midori' anthuriums are positioned in a way that creates plenty of layered depth. This time, the entire ring base has been covered, using various techniques including a pavé with carnations and rolled leaves. Finally, the front and back points are connected with rings of green midolino and equisetum, adding still more depth and rhythm to the composition.

ROYAL
Flowers
Floral Adhesive
Bindwire
Aluminum Wire
Green Waterproof Tape
OASIS
FLORAL PRODUCTS

CHAPTER 8

# More Strategies for Testing & Competition



Aside from using the Sketch & Score Method to build your skills, to boost your confidence, and in general to be as well prepared as possible, here are a few more things to keep in mind when you are approaching a hands-on evaluation or floral design competition.

**Stick to the ground rules.** Across the board, in every "surprise package" challenge, all participants are given an identical set of flowers, foliage, containers and supplies. You may choose, from your allotment, which flowers and supplies to use in each design. Be careful, however, not to use any non-supplied materials. This will result in disqualification of the design in which they were used.

While you will likely be allowed to bring your own tools, usually, because of the facility, you will not be able to use hot glue, power tools, or color enhancements.

**Watch your mechanics.** Not only will the judges pay attention to the mechanics of your design, but in some cases, the evaluation may take place on the day after you have created your designs. Your concern should always be that your designs will appear as fresh as possible at the time of the evaluation.

**Manage your goals.** Since time will be limited, keep your designs on the simple side. You won't have time to plan and executive anything very elaborate, and complexity won't give you any extra points from the judges. On the contrary, it may serve only to bury your statement.

This book includes a glossary of design techniques that may enhance your work and help you adapt a template sketch by, for example, using layering to achieve more depth when the materials you are given require it. Some techniques are time consuming. If you plan to use any of these in a time-limited situation, be sure that you have practiced them to the point where you can execute them quickly and efficiently.

**Be ready to work with staples.** Ambitious designers often get their best inspiration from unusual materials: blooming cherry-blossom branches, jaw-dropping orchids or proteas, fresh tulips in the springtime. Or it might be the glaze on a new ceramic pot that fires your imagination.

In a surprise-package challenge, however, your thinking process for designing should follow the opposite direction. You have to plan your design according to the requested occasion and style, and then select your materials from among those supplied—and I can assure you that you probably will not get your "dream flowers." Instead, you will likely have staple florist flowers like roses, carnations, and lilies to work with, simply because the host organization probably has a limited budget for purchasing fresh flowers.

Indeed, the flowers are likely to be donated, and this may give you a clue in advance as to what will be made available. On one occasion, when I participated in a competition sponsored by the California Cut Flower Commission, I knew that I would likely receive in-season California-grown flowers, such as stock, larkspur, tulips, callas, snapdragons, and gladiolus (not typical competition materials). Having reviewed my design sketches in advance, I was able to make quick decisions about what to do with those flowers when I saw them as I entered the room.

When it comes to hard goods, suppliers usually donate the newest products on the market in order to promote them. So, it helps to be familiar with those products and think about how they can be used in advance.

Every situation is different, but the following chart may give a general idea of what flowers are likely or not likely to be available for designers in a testing or competition scenario.



| CATEGORY | MOST LIKELY | MAYBE | NOT LIKELY |
|---|---|---|---|
| Fresh flowers - Mass flower | Rose<br>Carnation<br>Spray rose<br>Gerbera daisy<br>Calla lily<br>Asiatic lily<br>Button mum<br>Hypericum berry | Hydrangea<br>Stock<br>Tulip<br>Lisianthus<br>Sunflower<br>Chrysanthemum<br>Mini carnation<br>Aster | Hyacinth<br>Hellebore<br>Ranunculus |
| Fresh flowers - line flower | Gladiolus<br>Bells of Ireland<br>Liatris | Snapdragon<br>Larkspur | |
| Fresh flowers - filler flower | | Statice<br>Limonium | Gypsophila<br>Wax flower |
| Tropical flowers | Dendrobium orchid | Anthurium<br>Pin cushion protea | Phalaenopsis orchid<br>Cymbidium orchid |
| Foliage | Flax<br>Aralia<br>Grass<br>Aspidistra<br>Galax<br>Ruscus | Equisetum<br>Salal | Foxtail<br>Ming fern<br>Baker fern<br>Ivy |
| Branches and other | Curly willow<br>Dried birch branch<br>River cane | Succulents<br>Small potted blooming plants<br>Fruits | Bamboo branch<br>Pussy willow<br>Blooming branch |

PROPERTY OF DVFC
Aluminum Wire
Floral Adhesive

# Essential Techniques

## To Know And Use

Certain design techniques are especially useful whenever you have limited time and material, as in competition or testing, but also in daily work. You will find examples of the following techniques throughout this book. Remembering and mastering them can make your designs stand out with a polished, sharp-edged look that offers plenty of depth and line interest. You can find further full and clear definitions of these techniques in *The AIFD Guide to Floral Design: Terms, Techniques, and Traditions*, pp.151-180.

### FOLIAGE MANIPULATIONS

• **Weaving** of materials like bear grass or lily grass can help you create pattern and add dimension to designs.

• **Braiding** is a kind of weaving that involves more than two strands of grass or any other material that can be woven.

• **Tailoring** is when you treat foliage like fabric: for example, removing parts of it for a cleaner look, or securing it in such a way that its natural shape is altered. Examples would include trimmed palm fronds and rolled leaves.

• **Sheltering** is another way to add depth to your designs. Usually, a broad leaf, elevated on its stem, is placed so that it partly covers a flower or grouping of flowers. This technique has the added appeal of pulling the viewer's eye into the design. It conveys a sense of security and of secrets revealed.

• **Shadowing** happens when flat materials like leaves or anthuriums are placed so that one appears like the shadow of the other, parallel to and beneath or behind it. Think of the effect in a sketch when the artist adds a shadow: there is no better way to create the feeling of depth and dimension.

• **Terracing** means what it sounds like: placing materials so that they create a stairstep pattern. It's a useful way of adding depth to the base of your design.

### WHAT TO DO WITH STEMS, TWIGS AND BRANCHES

Rarely will you be given flowering branches as part of a surprise package, but you might well receive curly willow, river cane or any kind of straight twigs. It's also possible to use stiff stems like carnation stems separately from the flowers. Any of these can be useful in adding line interest to designs and in creating support structures.

Two design techniques come especially into play here. They are similar and can be confused. Binding simply means tying materials together. Banding, technically, is purely decorative: it may be done to multiple stems or to a single stem, or even to the neck of a vase. What's important to remember is that in either case, the finished result, if it is visible, must be clean and precise.

### WHAT TO DO WITH WIRES

Maybe you prefer to use all-natural materials only for your designs, and wire is not really your cup of tea. Nonetheless, skill with wire is critical for testing and competition, where depth and line value are paramount criteria. You will be given line flowers and other linear botanical materials, but in a limited supply. Likewise, you will only get so much wire. You will need to decide at the beginning what you want to use where. But you will find that in competition, decorative wire can be your best friend.

Wire, especially flat wire, can also be useful as a textural contrast to your organic material. If you have a container with a metallic sheen, wire can be used to integrate your floral materials with the container.

Some tips on working with decorative wire:
• **Swirling:** Working with 12-gauge aluminum wire, avoid making random swirls. Any curves or shapes you give to wire must reveal a clear intention.

• **Bending and angling:** Always use needle-nose pliers to make sharp and clean angles in 12-gauge aluminum wire.

• **Flat wire:** Use it as a statement base for a wristlet, necklace, or hairpiece, or cut it into small squares for an interesting accent. But be careful not to overwhelm the other elements of your design with the use of flat wire, as it is a bold and eye-catching material.

• **Bullion wire:** Use it for banding, form it into spheres, or crumple it, mash it down, and stretch it thin to create shimmering flat shapes.

## HOW TO USE GLUE

Remember that cold glue leaves a yellow residue after it dries. Even if it doesn't seem to show when you first apply it, if it is not entirely covered by the materials that you are gluing together, the yellow residue will be visible later on and will cost you points in judging.

• To make sure that cold glue adheres securely, apply it very thinly to both surfaces.

• Cold glue adheres better to fuzzy or porous surfaces. If you are gluing a flower or leaf to a very smooth and shiny surface, you may need to rough the surface up (if you can do so without marring the part that will be visible later on) or add a small piece of strongly adhesive tape that is textured on the non-adhesive side.

Design shown at AIFD National Symposium 2018 Partners' Expo to promote the book, *Asian Allure*

**Additional Resources**

*The AIFD Guide to Floral Design: Terms, Techniques, and Traditions.* Second Edition. A comprehensive reference guide, covering everything from design techniques and the principles and elements of design to care and handling and the cultural significance of various plant materials. Available at *www.aifd.org.*

*A Fresh Look at Judging Floral Design: A Guide for Judges, Designers, Teachers, Mentors and Hosts,* by Hitomi Gilliam AIFD and Kathy Whalen AIFD. With self-evaluation checklists, explorations of the psychology of creative design and evaluation, and much more. *https://judgingfloraldesign.com/book/*

# Product Credits

**Chapter 4: Formal Linear Design**

*Page 25, pink design with accents of flat cane*

**Fresh Materials:** pink snapdragons, gerbera daisies, fuchsia stock, carnations, Xanadu leaves, aspidistra leaves, aralia *(Fatsia japonica)*, white Oriental lily buds, Italian ruscus, mini green hydrangea, green hypericum berries, variegated lily grass

**Supplies:** a black cube container, OASIS® floral foam, OASIS® UGlu adhesive, OASIS® Flat Cane

*Page 28, design with birds of paradise*

**Fresh Materials:** birds of paradise, yellow 'Gelosia' roses, orange Asiatic lilies, belladonna delphinium, 'Yellow Babe' spray roses, yarrow, green hypericum berries, thistle, mini green hydrangea, croton leaves, 'Xanadu' philodendron leaves, ginger leaves, aspidistra leaves

**Supplies:** a black cube container, OASIS® Mega aluminum wire, OASIS® floral foam

*Page 30, yellow and orange design with curving aspidistra leaves*

**Fresh Materials:** sunflower, yellow button mums, 'Babe' spray roses, mini monstera leaves, croton leaves, variegated aspidistra, craspedia, green cymbidium, white football mum, yarrow, mini green hydrangea.

**Supplies:** OASIS® copper aluminum wire, OASIS® pear leaf natural wrap, OASIS® UGlu adhesive, 24-gauge florists' wire, wooden picks

*Page 34, red and yellow design with gingers, anthuriums, gerberas, yellow cymbidiums, and spray roses*

**Fresh Materials:** anthuriums, red gerbera daises, yellow button mums, red ginger, 'Mikado' red spray roses, yellow cymbidium orchids, red hypericum berries, Italian ruscus, anthurium leaves, birds of paradise leaves, variegated lily grass

**Supplies:** a white ceramic container, OASIS® red bullion wire, OASIS® floral adhesive, OASIS® floral foam

*Page 38, orange and yellow design with birds of paradise, orange roses, craspedia, flat wire*

**Fresh Materials:** birds of paradise, 'Free Spirit' roses, yarrow, craspedia, 'Green Trick' dianthus, green hypericum berries, croton leaves, 'Xanadu' philodendron leaves, variegated pittosporum, aspidistra leaves

**Supplies:** a two-tone ceramic container by Accent Décor, OASIS® floral foam, OASIS® flat copper aluminum wire, OASIS® floral adhesive

*Page 42, blue and white design with angled equisetum*

**Fresh Materials:** purple lisianthus, 'Eskimo' white roses, belladonna delphinium, solidago, 'Green Trick' dianthus, thistle, green cymbidium orchids, equisetum, a ginger leaf, aralia foliage, *Pittosporum tenuifolium*

**Supplies:** a ceramic pot, OASIS® floral foam, OASIS® 3/16" Flat Wire, OASIS® Aluminum Wire

*Page 45, design with river cane, snapdragons, and red lily*

**Fresh Materials:** a 'Starfighter' lily, snapdragons, hot pink carnations, 'Green Trick' dianthus, lily grass, mini monstera leaves, variegated aspidistra leaves, variegated pittosporum

**Supplies:** a five-inch gold mercury cube from Teleflora, OASIS® Aluminum Wire, river cane, OASIS® floral foam, OASIS® Bullion Wire

*Page 48, vertical design with yellow snapdragons, knotted grasses, leaf shapes in gold wire*

**Fresh Materials:** 'Eskimo' roses, snapdragons, yarrow, button mums, mini monstera leaves, variegated lily grass, mini green hydrangea, hypericum berries, calathea leaves, variegated pittosporum

**Supplies:** a gold cylinder container, OASIS® Etched Wire, OASIS® floral foam

*Page 52, vertical design with red roses and rectangles of red wire*

**Fresh Materials:** a 'Starfighter' lily, 'Freedom' roses, red anthuriums, white carnations, white snapdragons, white stocks, aralia *(Fatsia japonica)* leaves

**Supplies:** a Teleflora white cube container, OASIS® floral foam, OASIS® Aluminum Wire

*Page 54, vertical design with green grasses and angled green midollino*

**Fresh Materials:** green anthuriums, orange spray roses, green cymbidium orchids, millet, croton leaves, equisetum, mini monstera leaves, peach hypericum berries, variegated aspidistra

**Supplies:** OASIS® Midollino Sticks, a plastic square dish, OASIS® floral foam, OASIS® bullion wire

*Page 57, parallel design with yellow heliconia, purple stock, and orange gladiolus*

**Fresh Materials:** *Heliconia psittacorum,* orange Asiatic lilies, green carnation, 'Green Trick' dianthus, green hypericum berries, variegated pittosporum, anthurium leaves, green cymbidium orchids, 'Babe' spray rose, purple stock, orange gladiolus, croton leaves, mini green hydrangea, ginger leaves, birds of paradise, purple lisianthus

**Supplies:** a wooden box, OASIS® floral foam

*Page 60, parallel design with white snapdragons and yellow craspedia on the left, tailored ginger leaves and pale green gladiolus on the right*

**Fresh Materials:** craspedia, white Asiatic lilies, yarrow, 'Yellow Babe' spray roses, green gladiolus, 'Green Trick' dianthus, white snapdragons, belladonna delphinium, ginger leaves, green hypericum berries

**Supplies:** a wooden box, OASIS® floral foam

*Page 63, horizontal design with straws*

**Fresh Materials:** yellow 'Gelosia' roses, orange 'Babe' spray roses, white daisies, white dendrobium orchids, green button mums, yellow button mums, *Pittosporum tenuifolium,* 'Green Trick' dianthus

**Supplies:** OASIS® floral foam, plastic drinking straws, three Teleflora white cube containers

*Pages 66-67, horizontal design with flax leaves and flat wire*

**Fresh Materials:** variegated hala leaves, orange gerbera daisies, 'Cool Water' lavender roses, green carnations, Xanadu philodendron foliage, liatris, 'Babe' spray roses, 'Green Trick' dianthus, green hypericum berries

**Supplies:** OASIS® floral foam, OASIS® 1" Flat Wire, OASIS® 3/16" Flat Wire, three Teleflora white cube containers

*Pages 70-71, horizontal design with slanting red midollino, red roses, anthuriums*

**Fresh Materials:** red anthuriums, 'Freedom' red roses, 'Yellow Babe' spray roses, 'Green Trick' dianthus, mini green cymbidium orchids, red carnations, craspedia, mini green hydrangea, philodendron foliage, Italian ruscus, ming fern

**Supplies:** three Teleflora white cube containers, OASIS® floral foam, red OASIS® Midollino Sticks, OASIS® red bullion wire

*Pages 74-75, horizontal design with equisetum and mahogany bamboo*

**Fresh Materials:** equisetum, green cymbidium orchids, orange Asiatic lilies, 'Babe' spray roses, 'Green Trick' dianthus, mini green hydrangea

**Supplies:** three Teleflora white cube containers, OASIS® floral foam, bamboo sticks, river stone pebbles, OASIS® Bind Wire

*Page 76, curvilinear yellow design with silver mesh and silver wide flat wire*

**Fresh Materials:**yellow Asiatic lilies, 'Gelosia' yellow roses, yellow callas, craspedia, yarrow, white football mum, yellow cymbidium, variegated lily grass

**Supplies:** a rectangular glass vase, OASIS® Floral Mesh, OASIS® 1" Flat Wire

*Page 80, triangular L-Shaped design with tall stem of lily buds, red roses and ginger*

**Fresh Materials:** 'Freedom' roses, 'Mikado' spray roses, red ginger, white Oriental lily buds, white carnations, 'Xanadu' philodendron foliage, red ti leaves, anthurium leaves, variegated aspidistra

**Supplies:** a silver ceramic vase by Accent Décor, OASIS® floral foam, OASIS® silver flat aluminum wire, OASIS® bullion wire

**Chapter 5: Wedding Design**

*Page 87, green cascading bouquet with midollino*

**Fresh Materials:** green cymbidium orchids and carnations, white freesia, 'Green Ball' dianthus, ruscus foliage, aspidistra leaves

**Supplies:** a medium-size, straight-handle OASIS® Wedding Belle bouquet holder, OASIS® Midollino Sticks

*Page 90, cascading bouquet with red anthuriums and angled equisetum*

**Fresh Materials:** anthuriums, lily buds, mini green hydrangea, a philodendron leaf, equisetum, 'Green Ball' dianthus

**Supplies:** a medium-size, straight-handle OASIS® Wedding Belle bouquet holder, OASIS® bullion wire

*Page 94, red and white cascading bouquet with roses, orchids, and loops of lily grass*

**Fresh Materials:** white dendrobium orchids, white freesia, 'Freedom' roses, hypericum berries, lily grass, hypericum berries

**Supplies:** a medium-size, straight-handle OASIS® Wedding Belle bouquet holder

*Page 98, bouquet with copper flat wire*

**Fresh Materials:** croton leaves, button mums, carnations, gerbera daisy, 'Free Spirit' roses, 'Babe' spray rose, hypericum berries, 'Yellow Babe' spray roses, mini green hydrangea

**Supplies:** an OASIS® petite Wedding Belle bouquet holder, OASIS® Floral Adhesive, OASIS® Flat Wire

*Pages 102-103, bouquet with silver flat cane*

**Fresh Materials:** 'Free Spirit' roses, orange tulips, 'Babe' spray roses, carnations, Italian ruscus, chrysanthemums, cymbidium orchids

**Supplies:** an OASIS® petite Wedding Belle bouquet holder, faux variegated aspidistra, OASIS® bullion wire, OASIS® Flat Cane, birch-bark tape

*Page 106, bouquet with knotted lily grass, aluminum wire leaf shapes*

**Fresh Materials:** hot pink roses and tulips, green carnations, anthurium, stock, monstera leaf, variegated lily grass, variegated pittosporum

**Supplies:** an OASIS® petite Wedding Belle bouquet holder, faux variegated aspidistra ribbon, OASIS® Aluminum Wire

# Product Credits

*Page 108, handtied bouquet with circle of white carnations*

**Fresh Materials:** callas, carnations, lily grass, cymbidium orchids, Italian ruscus, mini monstera leaf, myrtle

**Supplies:** OASIS® Aluminum Wire, satin ribbon, floral tape

*Page 112, handtied bouquet with pink gerberas, long triangle-shaped extensions with pink wire*

**Fresh Materials:** pink gerbera daisies, pink veronica, aspidistra, Italian ruscus, green carnations, salal, white hydrangea

**Supplies:** OASIS® Aluminum Wire, OASIS® Bullion Wire

*Page 114, handtied bouquet with light green hypericum berries on wire stems*

**Fresh Materials:** hot pink roses and spray roses, purple carnations, Aralia *(Fatsia japonica)* leaves, variegated lily grass, green hypericum berries, millet, green cymbidium orchids, mini green hydrangea

**Supplies:** OASIS® Aluminum Wire, floral tape.



*Page 116, handtied yellow bouquet with sunflowers and star-shaped armature made of carnation stems*

**Fresh Materials:** sunflowers, 'Gelosia' yellow roses, white freesia, variegated pittosporum, 'Yellow Babe' spray roses, white carnations, yellow button mums

**Supplies:** OASIS® Bind Wire, satin ribbon

**Chapter 6: Flowers To Wear**

*Page 121, wrist corsage with wire leaves incorporating dusty miller*

**Fresh Materials:** dusty miller, white dendrobium orchids, white spray roses, equisetum, Italian ruscus

**Supplies:** OASIS® Flat Wire, OASIS® Diamond Wire, OASIS® Floral Adhesive

*Page 122, wrist corsage with white dendrobium orchids and silver wire*

**Fresh Materials:** white dendrobium orchids, white button mums, Italian ruscus.

**Supplies:** OASIS® Flat Wire, OASIS® Etched Wire, OASIS® Floral Adhesive

*Page 124, wrist corsage with yellow spray rose*

**Fresh Materials:** 'Yellow Babe' spray rose, lily grass, hypericum berries

**Supplies:** OASIS® Flat Wire, OASIS® Etched Wire, OASIS® Floral Adhesive

*Page 126, boutonniere with fuchsia dendrobium and reed "chopsticks" on an open rectangle of variegated artificial foliage*

**Fresh Materials:** variegated lily grass, purple dendrobium orchids

**Supplies:** cardboard, faux variegated aspidistra, OASIS® Aluminum Wire, OASIS® Bullion Wire, OASIS® Floral Adhesive

*Page 128, boutonniere with coiled decorative wire*

**Fresh Materials:** green hypericum berries, a white daisy, a yellow button mum

**Supplies:** OASIS® Aluminum Wire, OASIS® Floral Adhesive

*Page 130, rectangular boutonniere with orange and blue petals at the top*

**Fresh Materials:** bird-of-paradise petals, a green button mum, a croton leaf, orange gerbera daisy petals, orange hypericum berries

**Supplies:** cardboard, OASIS® Bullion Wire, OASIS® Aluminum Wire, OASIS® Floral Adhesive

*Page 133, necklace with white gerbera, coils of Diamond Wire*

**Fresh Materials:** a white daisy, a yellow mum, white larkspur, pothos foliage

**Supplies:** OASIS® Diamond Wire, OASIS® Metallic Wire, OASIS® Bullion Wire, OASIS® Floral Adhesive

*Page 136, blue necklace with green cymbidium orchid*

**Fresh Materials:** mini green cymbidium orchid, thistle, green hypericum berries, lily grass, green button mums, light blue delphinium florets

**Supplies:** OASIS® Aluminum Wire, OASIS® Floral Adhesive

*Page 138, fuchsia necklace with dendrobium orchid, wavy wire*

**Fresh Materials:** dendrobium orchids, gomphrena, waxflower, Italian ruscus

**Supplies:** OASIS® Aluminum Wire, OASIS® Bullion Wire, OASIS® Floral Adhesive

*Pages 140-141, hair piece*

**Fresh Materials:** spray roses, gomphrena, waxflowers, croton leaves

**Supplies:** OASIS® 3/16" Flat Wire, OASIS® Floral Adhesive

## Chapter 7: Sympathy Design

*Page 147, standing easel design with white lilies and purple iris*

**Fresh Materials:** white lilies, iris, liatris, gladiolus, white snapdragons, green carnations, lavender chrysanthemums, lily grass, philodendron and aralia leaves

**Supplies:** OASIS® Bullion Wire, OASIS® Tribute Cage® Holder

*Page 150, standing easel design with orange and purple flowers*

**Fresh Materials:** birds of paradise, large monstera leaves, orange gerbera daisies, 'Free Spirit' roses, orange snapdragons, purple dendrobium orchids, equisetum, aspidistra and monstera leaves.

**Supplies:** OASIS® Flat Wire, OASIS® Tribute Cage® Holder

*Page 152, standing easel design with red flowers plus white dendrobiums*

**Fresh Materials:** red ginger, anthuriums, 'Freedom' roses, red carnations, white dendrobiums; bird-of-paradise, anthurium, aspidistra and aralia foliage; lily grass, *Asparagus plumosus*

**Supplies:** OASIS® Tribute Cage® Holder

*Page 156, standing easel design with white lilies, yellow roses, curly willow arch*

**Fresh Materials:** yellow roses, craspedia, white lilies, carnations, and gladious, curly willow, a palm frond and other foliages

**Supplies:** artificial butterflies, OASIS® Tribute Cage® Holder

*Page 158, standing easel design with birds of paradise, orange gerberas, and large monstera leaf*

**Fresh Materials:** birds of paradise, orange gerberas and carnations, gladiolus, a monstera leaf, flax leaves, *Asparagus plumosus*

**Supplies:** rivercane, OASIS® Diamond Wire

*Page 160, wreath with purple and orange flowers, white lilies at the center*

**Fresh Materials:** liatris, orange gladiolus, white lilies, 'Free Spirit' roses, 'Babe' spray roses, orange carnations, purple dendrobiums, Aralia *(Fatsia japonica)* leaves, Israeli ruscus, aspidistra, myrtle

**Supplies:** OASIS® Wreath Base

*Page 162, wreath with yellow diagonal*

**Fresh Materials:** yellow Asiatic lilies, 'Gelosia' yellow roses, craspedia, 'Yellow Babe' spray roses, carnations, hala, ming fern, aspidistra, ginger leaves

**Supplies:** OASIS® Aluminum Wire, OASIS® Wreath Base

*Page 164, green and white wreath*

**Fresh Materials:** white gerbera daisies, 'Green Tea' roses, cymbidiums, carnations, aspidistra, ming fern, lily grass, white dendrobium orchids, Italian ruscus, white callas, mini green hydrangea, millet, hypericum, anthurium leaves, 'Snowflake' mini roses, 'Green Trick' dianthus, dracaena leaves, equisetum.

**Supplies:** OASIS® Wreath Base

*Pages 168-169, casket top with yellow and white flowers, angled hala leaves*

**Fresh Materials:** yellow Asiatic lilies, white football mums, white carnations, ginger leaves, yellow roses, hala leaves, variegated aspidistra, palm fronds, white gladiolus, white gerbera daisy, variegated lily grass, white snapdragons, a monstera leaf, equisetum

**Supplies:** OASIS® floral foam in a casket saddle, 16-gauge floral wire

*Pages 172-173, casket spray with rolled variegated ginger leaves, red Flat Wire, red roses and anthuriums*

**Fresh Materials:** ginger leaves, 'Freedom' roses, red anthuriums, red carnations, lavender carnations, purple larkspur, purple dendrobium orchids, variegated aspidistra, anthurium leaves, Aralia *(Fatsia japonica)*, myrtle



**Supplies:** OASIS® floral foam in a casket saddle, OASIS® 3/16" Flat Wire

*Page 176, cremation urn design with purple and white flowers*

**Fresh Materials:** aspidistra leaves, gladiolus, carnations, liatris, callas, lily grass, palm leaves, white roses,

**Supplies:** OASIS® Midollino Sticks, OASIS® Ring Holder

*Page 178, cremation urn design with green and white flowers*

**Fresh Materials:** 'Midori' anthuriums, cymbidiums, 'Green Tea' roses, carnations, ginger leaves, mini green hydrangea, equisetum, hypericum berries, ming fern, philodendron leaves

**Supplies:** OASIS® Midollino Sticks, OASIS® Ring Holder

Design created for presentation at Portland, Oregon's Lan Su Chinese Garden, 2018

# Acknowledgments

The idea for this book has been simmering ever since I started teaching floral design. It took a while to really formulate a method that I could use to help my students in the way that I wanted to do. The goals and the method might seem daunting or intimidating to some. But I hope the contents of this book will be encouraging to anyone who truly wants to improve their design skills and their "design eyes." My purpose is to help you step up when it comes to the participating in floral design competitions, professional evaluations, or your daily surprise package.

I owe a huge debt to my editor, co-writer, and adviser Bruce Wright for his help in completing this book. The best step I took was to lure him to become involved in this project. He genuinely understands my ideas and designs and re-wrote every sentence that I struggle with the most. Lots of the conceptual teaching in this book was able to be shaped thanks to his thorough expertise in floral design and the floral industry.

I also owe big-time to my publisher, Travis Rigby, who trusted in me when I didn't have a big reputation. Thanks to his full support, I was able to get my first book published in 2018: *Asian Allure,* co-authored with Greg Lum AIFD, EMC and Lily Chan AIFD, EMC. After that, when I approached Travis about this book, he agreed to publish it even before he had seen any designs. At Wildflower Media, book designer Kathleen Dillinger was also of tremendous help in lifting up the quality of the book and helping me to realize my vision.

This beautiful book wouldn't be possible without the beautiful photography of Bianca Madanat! Bianca has been working with me on all of my photography needs for a while now. This kind of collaboration was only possible because she is not only a fantastic photographer, but also a wonderful florist herself. Thank you, Bianca, for your patience with me.

I thank my business partner Teleflora, especially Lottie McKinnon and Michael Martin, for their support of my project and their support for floral industry education in general. I am grateful also to Smithers-Oasis for their generous support as well. Many of my AIFD "family" have been supportive of this project too.

I must thank the staff and students at Park Florist and Washington Flower School—people that I work with every day who actually helped me try out and test my teaching method. They are the true testimonials of this book! Thank you, Wynne, Rosana, Jeena, Sarah, Elise, for gluing me down when I was afloat with my crazy ideas and helping me get down to work.

Lastly but not least, I want to express my sincere appreciation and love for my family, who encouraged me to finish my journey on this book. Love you, Dennis, Joanne, Chris, Ian, and Mom!

—Jeanne Ha AIFD, CFD

## ABOUT THE AUTHOR

Jeanne Ha, AIFD, CFD, is the owner of a successful retail florist business and a founder and instructor of a school for the teaching of floral design and business. She is internationally recognized as a floral designer and as an AIFD Certified Floral Evaluator/Judge.

Owner of Park Florist in Takoma Park, Maryland, since 2004, she cofounded Washington Flower School, also in Takoma Park, in 2010.

In that same year (2010), she was inducted as a member of the American Institute of Floral Designers. Since then, she has been a featured designer and presenter at a number of educational programs across the country, from Washington, D.C. to Oregon. Design awards in competition include the first place for floral jewelry in the Sylvia Cup Design Competition in 2014 and the grand prize (first place) in the Potomac Floral Wholesale Flower Design Show in 2019.

Jeanne has served as President for the Teleflora MD-VA-DC Unit in 2015-2016 and 2020-2021. She has been a board member with the Unit since 2014.



Jeanne's shop, Park Florist, has been featured in SAF's *Floral Management* magazine, in *Flowers& Magazine*, and in the Korean florist magazine *floral*.

In 2018, Jeanne co-authored the book *Asian Allure: A Compilation of Inspirational Creations from Prominent Asian Designers*, which also featured work by Greg Lum AIFD EMC and Lily Chan AIFD EMC. In *Florists' Review*, 2020-2021, she contributed the design columns "Ready, Set, Design."

Trained as a classical musician, Jeanne completed both a bachelor's degree (with a major in voice) and a master's degree (with a major in musicology) at Seoul National University in Seoul, South Korea. She went on to complete course work at the College of Music, University of Maryland, in College Park, Maryland.

## ABOUT THE EDITOR

Bruce Wright served as an editor at *Flowers& Magazine*, published by Teleflora, from 1982 to 1994, and again from 1997 to 2018, when the magazine ceased publication. In 1992, he received AIFD's Award of Merit Industry. He is currently active as an independent journalist and editor at *www.brucewrites.com*.